SEOUL, KOREA

TO GIVE
ANYTHIN[G]
THAN YOU[]
IS TO SA[Y]
THE GIFT[]

G LESS

UR BEST

CRIFICE

—STEVE PREFONTAINE
AMERICAN DISTANCE RUNNER

QUITO, ECUADOR

THE DAY THE WORLD STOPPED TO RUN

THE+
HUMAN
RACE
10K

TEXT EDITED BY
BOB ROE

PHOTOGRAPHY EDITED BY
JAY COLTON

DESIGNED BY
KARLSSONWILKER INC.

PRODUCED BY

MELCHER MEDIA

Published by

124 West 13th Street
New York, NY 10011
www.melcher.com

Publisher: Charles Melcher
Associate Publisher: Bonnie Eldon
Editor in Chief: Duncan Bock

Executive Editor: Lia Ronnen
Associate Editor: Lauren Nathan
Editorial Assistant: Coco Joly
Production Director: Kurt Andrews
Production Assistant: Daniel del Valle

Web site Editors: David Brown and Jessi Rymill

This book was produced using Forest Stewardship Council certified paper and printing.

© 2008 Nike. All rights reserved.

Photographs © by individual photographers listed on pages 254–255

Illustrations by karlssonwilker inc.

Front and back cover photographs by Nicolas Goldberg

All rights reserved.
No part of this publication may be reproduced,
stored in a retrieval system, or transmitted in any
form or by any means, electronic, mechanical,
photocopying, recording, or otherwise,
without prior consent of the publishers.

12 11 10 09 08   10 9 8 7 6 5 4 3 2 1

Printed in the U.S.A.
ISBN: 978-1-59591-051-6

Library of Congress Control Number: 2008938118

Nike will donate a minimum of $25,000 to the Lance Armstrong Foundation and a minimum of $25,000 to UN refugee agency's **nine**million.org campaign. Nike will donate a fixed amount of $25,000 to WWF.

FOREWORD ALBERTO SALAZAR	022
RUN FOR YOUR LIFE DON KARDONG	028
RUNNING FOR A CAUSE FRANZ LIDZ	094
THE MAKING OF A RACE E. CASEY KITTRELL	202
YOU'LL NEVER RUN ALONE AGAIN	212
AFTERWORD: WHY WE RUN KENNY MOORE	240
COURSE MAPS	246
ABOUT THE CONTRIBUTORS	252
PHOTOGRAPHY CREDITS	254
ACKNOWLEDGMENTS	256

LIMA, PERU

FOREWORD

We make our own choices. Most of us choose to act—to participate and compete and achieve. We are driven to find a role in the greater good. All we need is a way to share our passion and chase our potential—a paintbrush, a tenor sax, a farmer's work ethic, a book of faith, a nurturing soul. For some of us, all we need is a pair of lungs and a piece of open ground. We choose to run.

On August 31, 2008, hundreds of thousands of us pushed aside the complexities of life to join a global 10K run called The Nike+ Human Race. In Istanbul, we ran across the Bosporus Bridge connecting Europe and Asia. President Ma Ying-Jeou of Taiwan led thousands of us from Taipei City Hall to Dajia Riverside Park. Thousands of people ran on the streets of Los Angeles, one of us proclaiming for his team, "We're not gonna win, but we're gonna finish!" We ran past the Palace of Culture and Science in Warsaw, along Singapore's Shenton Way, through Tel Aviv with minister Ami Ayalon and his three sons. In Austin and Buenos Aires and London and New York City, we ran, 25 cities in all, along with thousands more around the world. It was an unprecedented celebration of the running community, and every step went to benefit The Lance Armstrong Foundation, UNHCR, the UN Refugee Agency's ninemillion.org campaign and the WWF. "Just do it," on a global scale.

There were no prerequisites. Everybody ran. Young and old. Fast and slow. The known and unknown. World champions ran shoulder to shoulder with first-timers. Everybody qualified. This is the nature of The Nike+ Human Race—democracy snapping its political roots to rise above culture and geography and unite people around the world in miles of moments shared.

There is irony in the idea of a communal run, because we all run for our own reasons. We run in our heads. We run with our spirit. As the muscle warms and the stiffness fades, we run with a rhythm all our own. We run toward some things and away from others—ultimately we run alone.

But solidarity is stronger than solitude. As with every authentic community, insights run deep. Asked once to define jazz, a legendary trumpet player replied, "If you have to ask, you'll never know." That's how it is with running. It's something everyone can grasp intellectually; and yet, to really know its beauty you have to embrace it in full—every challenge and finish, the beat downs and boredom, and the joy of achievement, those moments at the end of a run with our hands on our hips and sweat dripping off our chin, running farther than ever before, feeling like we could run forever, and the sweet soreness that makes us know we're alive. That's how it is with runners. And so it is with the human race.

**—Alberto Salazar,
Running Icon**

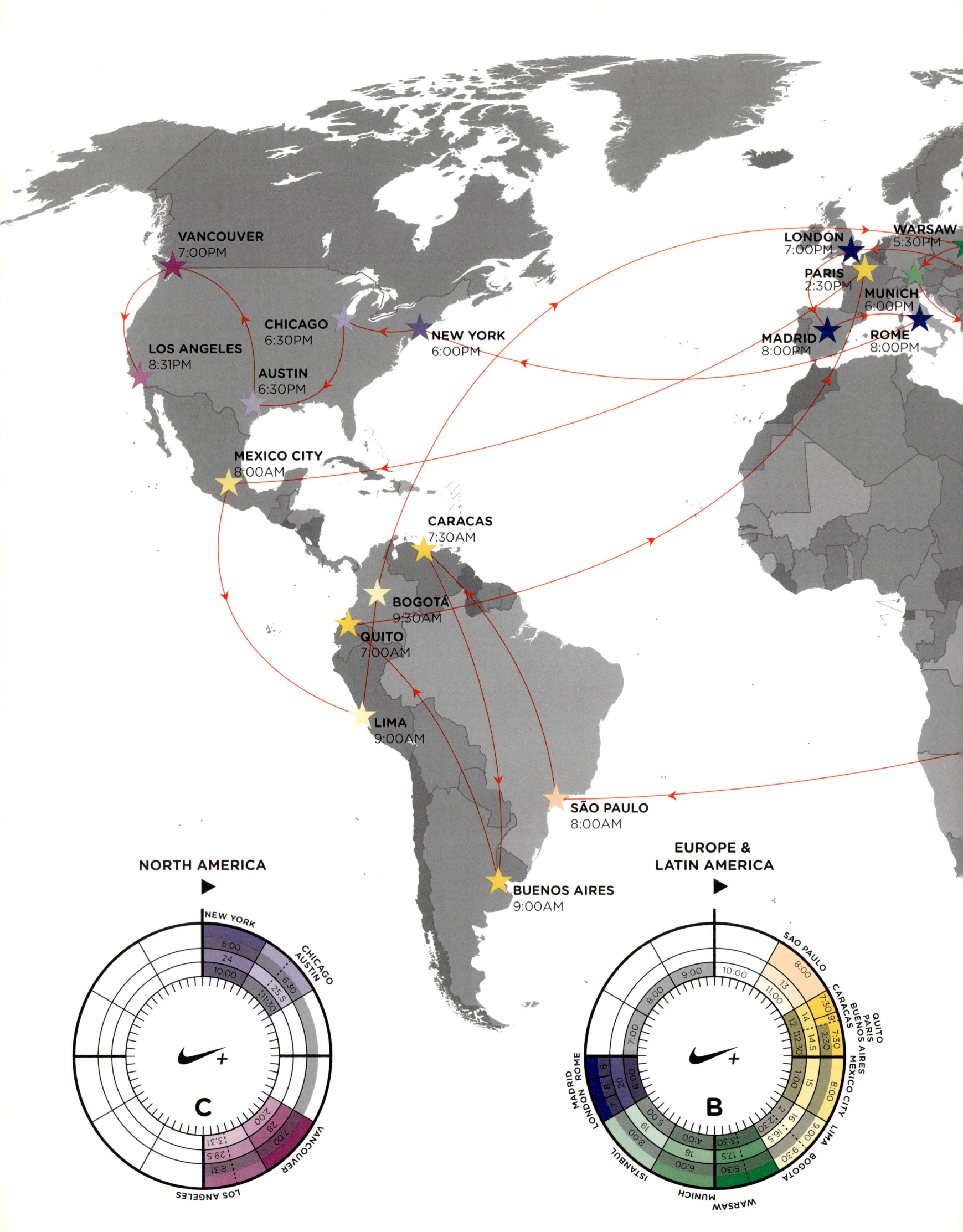

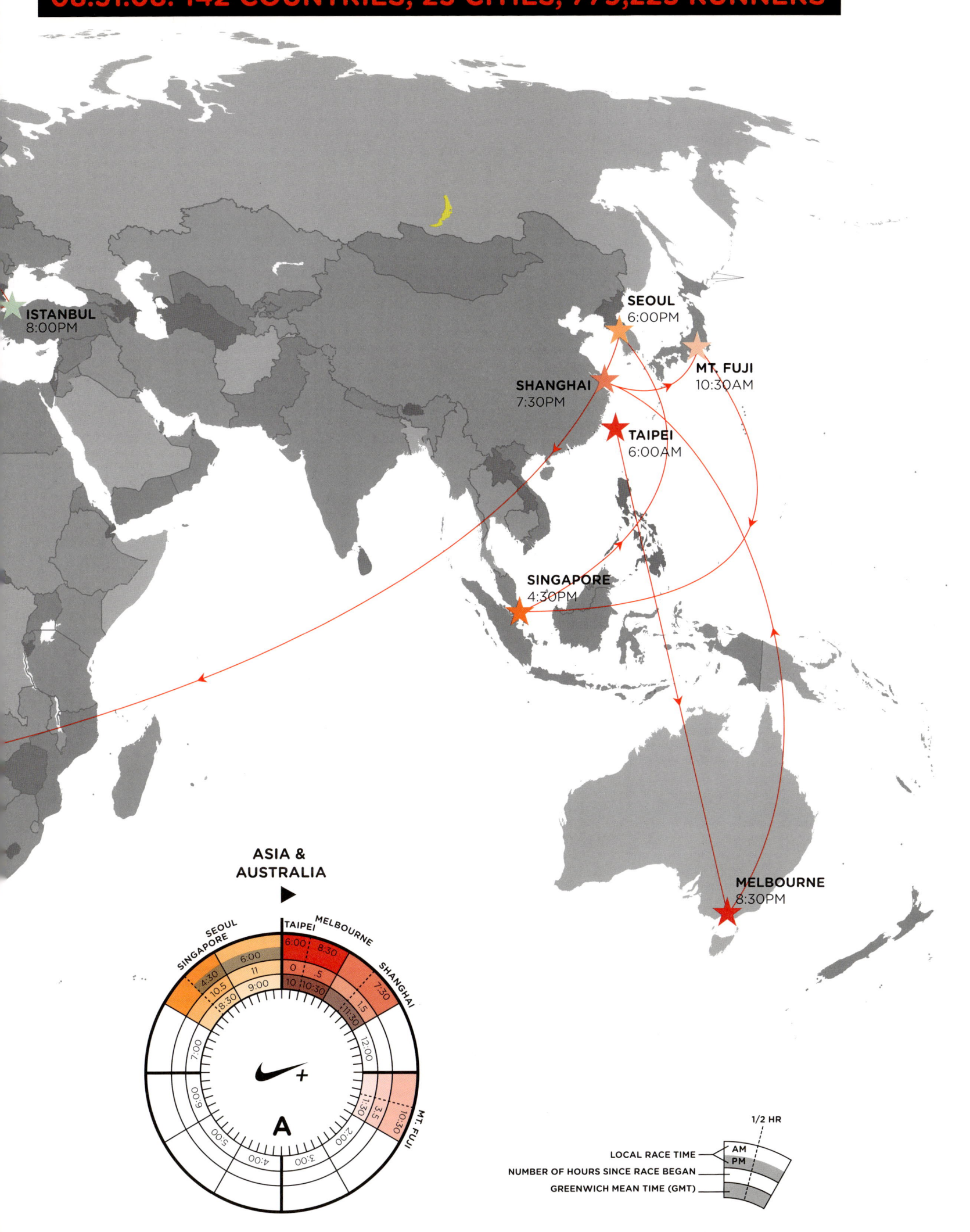

RUN FOR YOUR LIFE

As a high school sophomore, I took the road less traveled. I joined the cross-country team, where I learned that running is a great instructor for anyone willing to sign up for the course.

We were, by and large, outcasts—geeks and dorks and skinny oddballs with pale legs sticking out of baggy PE shorts. I attended an all-boys school, a football powerhouse, and in the fall any student with an urge to belong and a body that could take a pounding was slamming pads and banging helmets. Cross-country, on the other hand, functioned only as a conditioning activity for other sports, which is why I joined. When you have basketball aspirations and the basketball coach suggests you turn out for cross-country, you don't tell him you have no idea what cross-country is. You turn out.

I wasn't totally clear about what "cross-country" meant, but I got running. I had watched TV footage of a man running barefoot in Rome in 1960, and his performance was riveting—26 miles, for God's sake. Barefoot. An impossible journey, it seemed, but he ran easy as the wind, self-assured, even regal. I was entranced, but I didn't dare dream of doing anything like that. I was a teenager and prone to fantasy, but I had a clear notion of the size of the world.

My first workout was on a Thursday—we were a couple dozen acolytes with no clear notion of what was ahead. Our coach directed us to run to Green Lake, a little over three miles away, which was a daunting start to the afternoon. Once there he shepherded us through five "interval miles" on the public track. Afterward, legs still wobbly from this first crushing speed session of our young lives, my friend Pat and I jogged halfway back to school before the full measure of our decision to turn out for cross-country filled our calves and hamstrings like cement. We walked the final mile.

A weekend was plenty of time for 15-year-old legs to recover, though, and the next week we were back at it. We ran hill repeats, long runs through "the ravine," speed-drills in the park and a diabolical variety of other workouts that steadily reshaped our bodies, not to mention our psyches. We began boasting that we worked harder than the football team. Of course, we only boasted to each other.

There was a reservoir in the park a mile from school with a dirt path around it, where we did speed-work. "On the line. Go!" Coach would shout, sending us racing around the 300-meter circuit. Then it was "Keep jogging!" as our chests heaved afterward, struggling for air while we swallowed the slight but unmistakable taste of blood. Who knew from where that taste emanated? Lungs? Stomach? And, always before we were ready, "On the line. Go!" Around again. And again. And again. Other teenagers, we knew, weren't doing this. Wouldn't do this. It hurt like hell, but as our legs emptied of energy our spirits soared. We were tough!

So yes, we reveled in our training and embraced being different. We dyed our gray sweats orange, lime green, raspberry, pink. "Jeez," said one classmate, "You cross-country runners are a bit on the odd side."

Odd for sure, but we were winning meets, and athletic fame trumps a lot in the teenage world. That was the best thing about cross-country, maybe the first lesson I learned from running. Hard work matters. If you do the work, you'll get better. If you don't, you won't.

As I whittled myself into shape, I awakened a talent I didn't know I possessed. And each week, I moved steadily up the team food chain. Heading into the big meet at the end of the season, I was close to the top.

The day before that meet, our coach took us to a spot a few hundred meters from the finish line. There, a spur off the main footpath around the lake veered closer to the shoreline. It was a shortcut, but just barely, and it was narrower and rockier than the main route. "The other runners are going to take the shortcut," he said. "But stay on the main path, which has better footing, and start your kick here."

The next morning, I dogged the heels of more experienced runners, and sure enough, they took the shortcut. I stayed on the main trail and sprinted like crazy, trying to channel the distance runner I had seen on TV sprinting to glory in Tokyo. When the paths merged a few meters later, I was in the lead, and I stayed there, racing to the first victory of my running career.

I passed that spot many times in the years that followed, and eventually I realized that my coach's tip had nothing to do with better footing. Either path would have been fine. I won that race because I believed I could. And that's another lesson running taught and continues to teach, whether you're running a marathon or your first 10K. Believe.

Combine hard work with self-confidence, and the individual thrives. That is the power of one. But in a sport where individual achievement is celebrated, I found the deepest satisfaction in running as part of a group. In college, I began to understand the power an individual can derive from those around him.

When I showed up for college, I was profoundly unprepared to run competitively. The summer after my senior year of high school had been loads of fun, but I hadn't done much training. In fact, I was ambivalent about competing any longer.

I turned out as a lark. How hard could it be, I wondered, to run on a freshman team that only competed against other freshmen teams? Well, it was plenty hard, but I was surrounded by teammates with high aspirations, and I wanted in. I showed up religiously every afternoon, and I steadily improved. High school reservoir workouts morphed into half-mile repeats on the school's golf course, long intervals with little rest and lots of moments when I asked myself, "Why was it, again, that I decided to do this?" I survived, though, and added morning workouts, a serious assault on my deeply held conviction that mornings are for snoozing. It's amazing what you can get yourself to do.

By the end of that year, I was one of the two top freshmen on our team. The two of us would later run together for the national team.

Surround yourself with great people—that's what I learned. Sophomore year we had a new coach, and a dynamic team captain. Those two nurtured a lofty vision of our potential. By the end of that season, we had worked our way from being an average Bay Area team to nearly taking home the title at the NCAA Cross-country Championships in New York. I was fourth man on the team, hanging on for dear life as we nabbed second place, nearly upsetting Villanova.

Yes, surround yourself with great people and you'll learn the power of more than one. Later in my running life, my partners have done many things—they've kept the pace honest, motivated me when my spirits are deflated, provided entertainment when our tails are dragging, prodded me back to fitness after a layoff. When it's zero degrees and they've promised to be there, they're there. So am I. You trust, and you strive to be trustworthy.

Of course, partners are hard to find. After graduating, I usually found myself training alone, and with no coach to provide direction. Just me, trying to keep a dream simmering.

Somehow it worked. When I finally reached the starting line of my biggest race, I stood there with an inner peace born of sweat. My confidence was earned, a precipitate of thousands of miles of preparation. And those miles were logged, as often as not, with legs drained, skies darkening, a warm house calling my name and the knowledge that 10 miles remained to be run. Strong coffee helped. Mostly, though, that was a time to measure determination. I discovered I could run 10 miles in the dark, or mile repeats in blazing hot weather until "the golden orb" appeared in my field of vision (a sure sign of dehydration). I could do whatever the day demanded.

Non-runners ask us where we get the motivation to train. If only they had motivation, they insist, they might be able to do it too. But motivation isn't something you have. It's something you summon. Or you don't.

This, of course, speaks of patience. Hard work matters, but it doesn't matter very quickly. Improvement comes from weeks, months, years of putting one foot in front of the other. If we don't already have patience, we learn it. Or we don't, and we are non-runners again. We've been called one-dimensional, dullards and worse, for holding the single thought of becoming the best runners we can be. I call it doggedness.

You learn humility, too. Not many years after running on the world stage, I was in the middle of a 10-mile run on icy streets, after dark, heading uphill and silently congratulating myself on my toughness, when a 16-year-old high school girl suddenly passed me. I've run 50 miles, raced up the stairwell to the top of the Empire State Building, run from one rim of the Grand Canyon to the other and back. And been passed by a young girl during training. "Don't look back," Satchel Page once said, "something might be gaining on you." In running, someone is always gaining on you. Today a 16-year-old girl, tomorrow a bald-headed guy 10 years your senior. You learn not to let it spoil the fun.

Non-runners think we run for health, but we don't, not really. We run for life. Yes, running burns calories and strengthens the cardiovascular system. It reduces depression and clears the head. It promotes creativity and sociability. But more than that, running gives us a reason to go outside in winter, breathe in fresh forest air, be amazed at clouds burning orange and gold at sunrise, watch an eagle wheeling overhead. Running also provides opportunities to scour the cobwebbed niches of our souls for nuggets of worth we'd otherwise never know we had. If you've ever run out of fuel and felt motivation belly-flop at the 20-mile mark of a marathon, but you somehow found the wherewithal to finish anyway, you know what I mean.

I don't measure myself by the watch much any more. I run four or five times a week, eager to absorb whatever the activity offers. When I run now, I don't feel much different than I did over four decades ago. On a good day, without the tyranny of the watch, I feel blessed to be moving with relative ease. On a bad day the discomfort is simply another obstacle to overcome. That hasn't changed much.

What has changed is the company I keep. As a sophomore, I took the road less traveled. Today that road is busy with foot traffic, in the U.S. and around the world, people being shaped and molded by the simple act of putting one foot in front of the other as quickly as possible.

Dorks, geeks, oddballs? No doubt, but you could also simply describe us as people who have heard a call to action, not from a coach but from within.

"On the line. Go!"

**—Don Kardong,
Marathoner**

RUNNER'S POLL

Runners were polled on race day rituals and how they measured up against their goals.

Data based on answers provided by Nike+ Human Race online survey respondents.

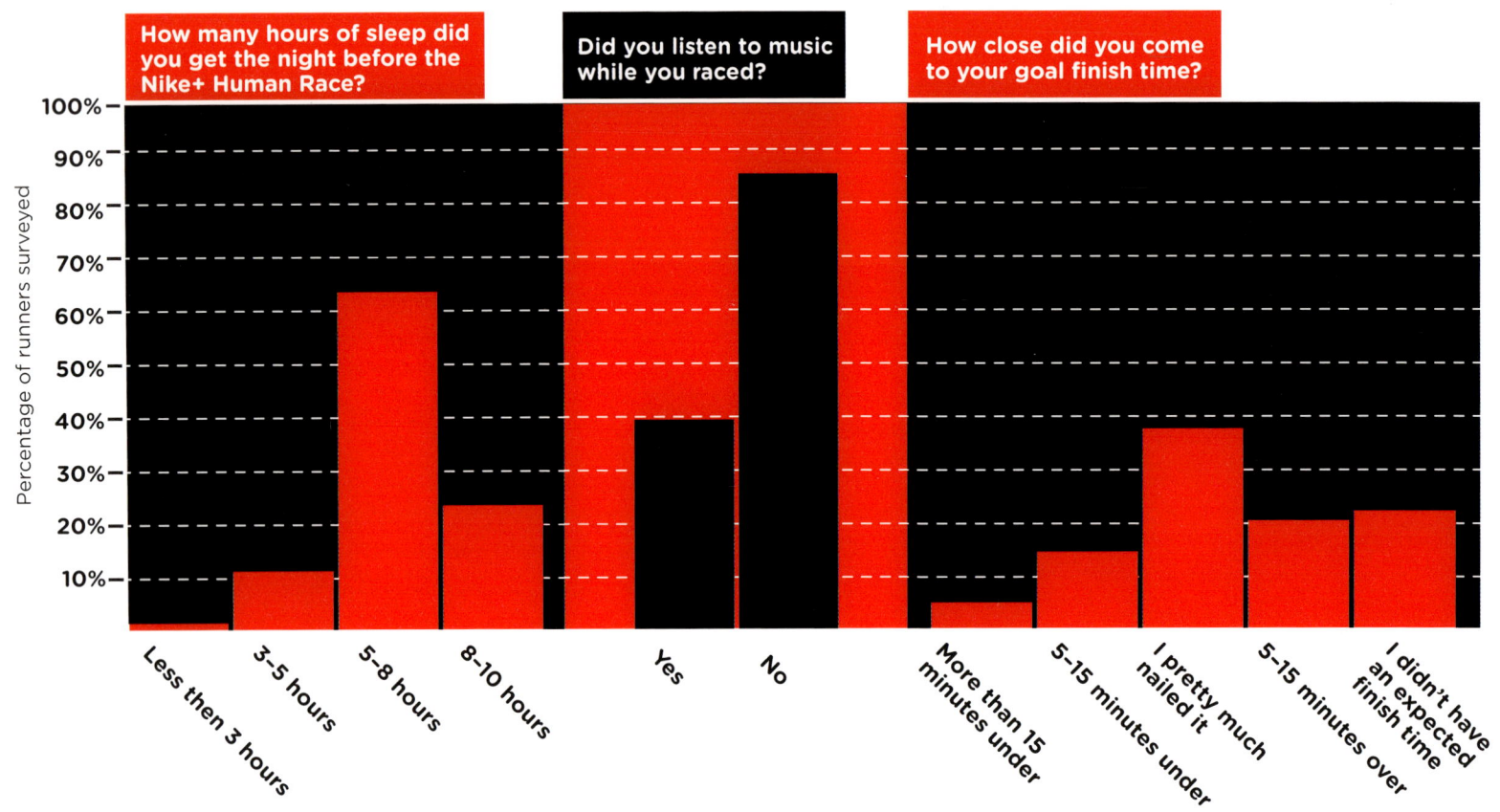

"I RUN BECAUSE…"

Text is courtesy of The Nike+ Human Race online survey respondents.

It's my Zen time. I want to beat my best time. I accomplish something every time I lace up my shoes. I come back home a mentally tougher person. One day I won't be able to. It makes me feel strong and sexy. God gave me long legs. The roads are always open. Endorphins don't come in pill form. It lets me be me. I am worth it. I must. I eat. I love the high. It reminds me I'm human. What else is there? I am the driver, I still can. I need to take care of myself for my wife and my kids. Life gives me the opportunity. I love to finish. The world seems simpler when I run. It gets me through my day.

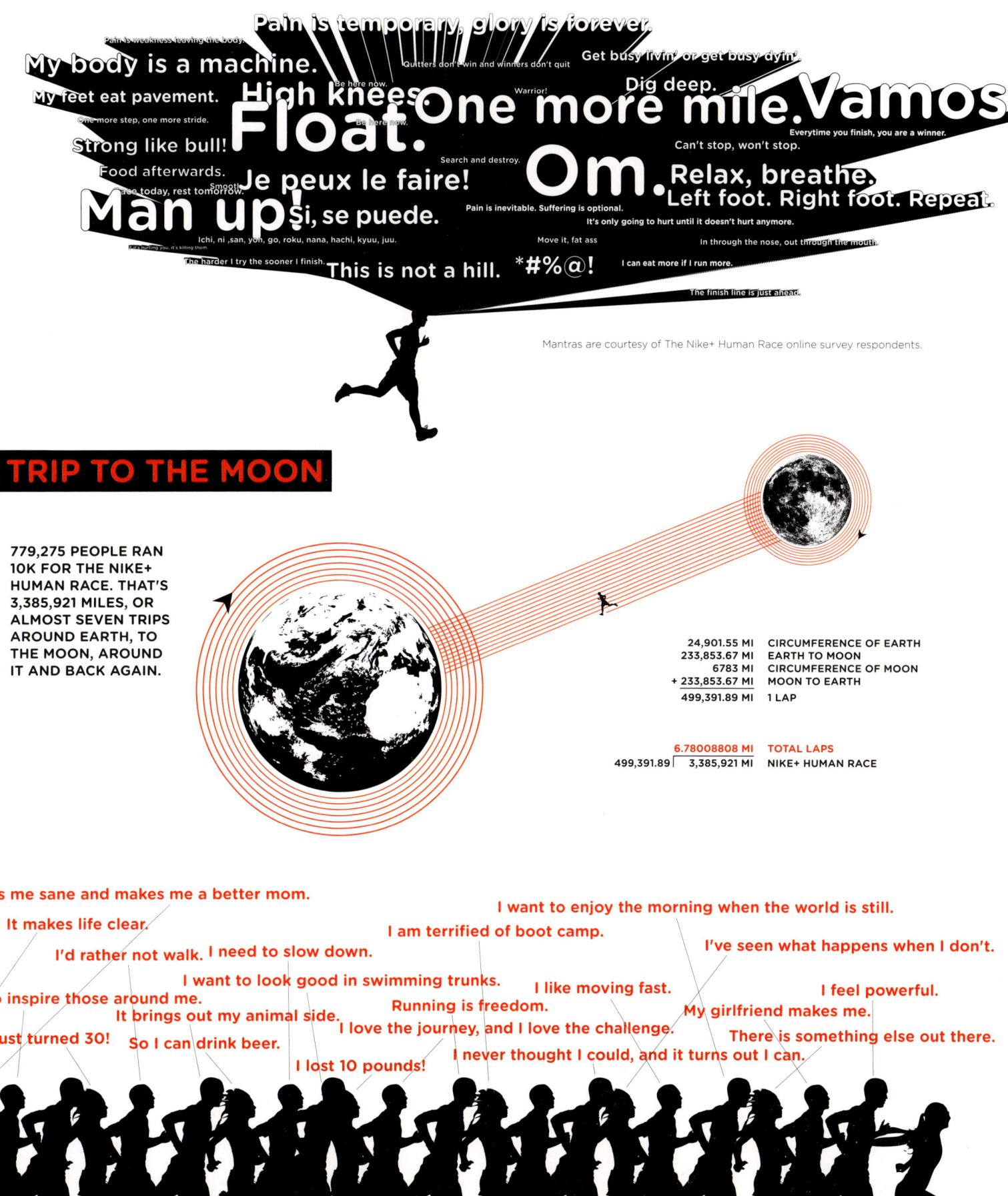

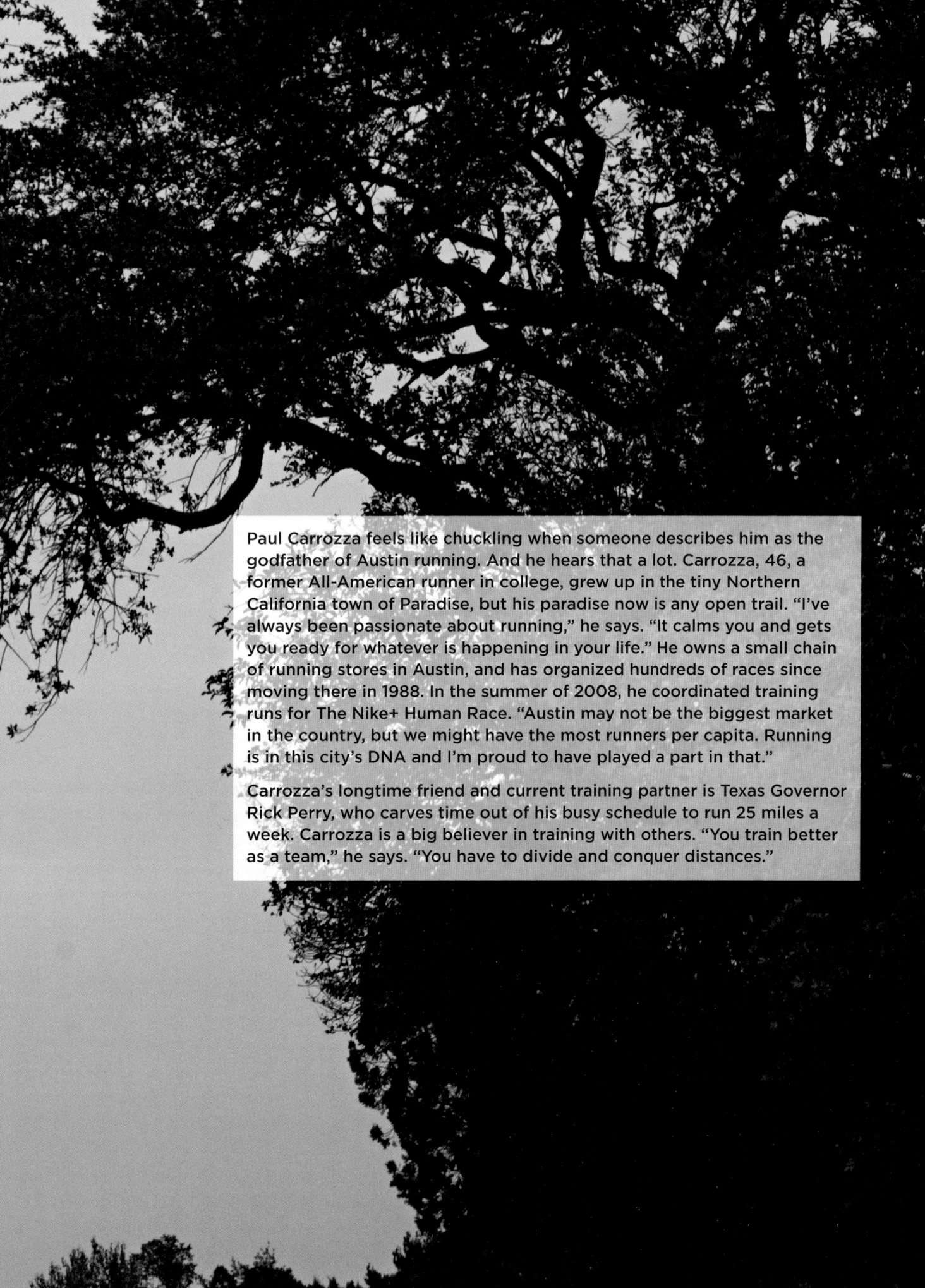

Paul Carrozza feels like chuckling when someone describes him as the godfather of Austin running. And he hears that a lot. Carrozza, 46, a former All-American runner in college, grew up in the tiny Northern California town of Paradise, but his paradise now is any open trail. "I've always been passionate about running," he says. "It calms you and gets you ready for whatever is happening in your life." He owns a small chain of running stores in Austin, and has organized hundreds of races since moving there in 1988. In the summer of 2008, he coordinated training runs for The Nike+ Human Race. "Austin may not be the biggest market in the country, but we might have the most runners per capita. Running is in this city's DNA and I'm proud to have played a part in that."

Carrozza's longtime friend and current training partner is Texas Governor Rick Perry, who carves time out of his busy schedule to run 25 miles a week. Carrozza is a big believer in training with others. "You train better as a team," he says. "You have to divide and conquer distances."

LORETO MANDEVILLE HALL TOORAK
NIKE+ SCHOOLS CHALLENGE
MELBOURNE, AUSTRALIA

Tam Brothwell, director of sport at Loreto Mandeville Hall Toorak in Melbourne, says entering her school in The Nike+ Schools Challenge made it a lot easier to persuade her students to exercise. With more than 130 high schools in Australia and New Zealand participating in the challenge, things got a little competitive—each school pulled together a team of 100 students, who used their Nike+ equipment to record their runs to see which school could put in the most training miles over 24 days. "It was a competition, but it was really a noncompetitive activity," says Jo Myers, who teaches at Kilbreda College. "It doesn't matter if the kid is not a fast runner, or if she can't run 10 kilometers in one go, so it didn't discriminate against those who aren't great athletes." Myers saw the benefits of the Challenge almost immediately. "Coming to school in the mornings I'd pass a lot of kids who decided to get off the train one station before their usual stop and were running or walking from there," she says.

Brothwell, who is an avid runner, says the Challenge was the perfect way for her students to get ready for The Nike+ Human Race. "Some of the girls would not have thought they were capable of running 10 kilometers, but after using their tracking devices and knowing that they had already been running those distances, they were confident they could finish. The race was amazing—what a positive way to end the Challenge for the Loreto Mandeville Hall girls!"

VICTOR RUBÉN GÓMEZ VERAZA
GRAPHIC DESIGNER
MEXICO CITY, MEXICO

"I train with four guys and two girls, and we all like to eat. After a morning workout we get breakfast, something spicy: quesadillas, eggs with chili sauce. I love the spiciest chilies in Mexico, which send sparks around my mouth, but I have to watch it the day before a big run. If I eat spicy tacos and other great Mexican dishes, I'm pretty useless in the race.

"I am happy to say that I felt really good in The Human Race and that my time was five minutes better than last year's. I've obviously been keeping in shape and eating right."

"At first we named ourselves 'See Jane Run,' but we called each other 'the Janes,' so that name stuck. It was cute and catchy, and it captured the spirit of what we do: give moms who'd been competitive runners a way to pursue the sport they love. I'm 42 now, and a mom; until I hit my 30s, running was my life—I ran in the U.S. trials in 1996. About six years ago, four of the original Janes asked me to develop a workout program for them. I suggested we form a running club so that we could all get back in shape and race. We now compete all over the country, and we've won two national championships. The main thing our group gives us is camaraderie and support. You want to run with women who understand what you're facing, as a runner and as a mother. We're recruiting women out of college—we try to show them they can have their family and career and run too."

"The day they handed out endurance, every member of my family was in line except me. In high school, I was a sprinter. My great-grandmother Ida started to run when she was 73—a year later, she ran her first marathon and became known as the Galloping Grandma. In 1990, she ran the Chicago Marathon in 6:53:50, which stood as the world record for women 85 years and older until last year. My great-grandmother, my grandfather and my father once ran a marathon together—three generations in the same race. My grandfather Sabba was also an avid runner.

"My goal was to become a world-class speed skater. But after five years of training, I was burned-out and hung up my skates. That changed last year after Starbucks asked me to be an advocate for The Human Race (I'm a barista there). I started to train five or six days a week. A 10-minute run used to be more than enough for me—now I can run 10 miles and not step on my tongue. Also, my competitive fire came back. In September, I plan to move from Chicago to Deer Valley, Utah, which is close to the U.S. Speed Skating training facility.

"I ran The Human Race to support the WWF, and if I achieve my goal, the race will have helped me, too. The race means different things to different people, but how many of the runners can say that it gave them the chance to dream again?"

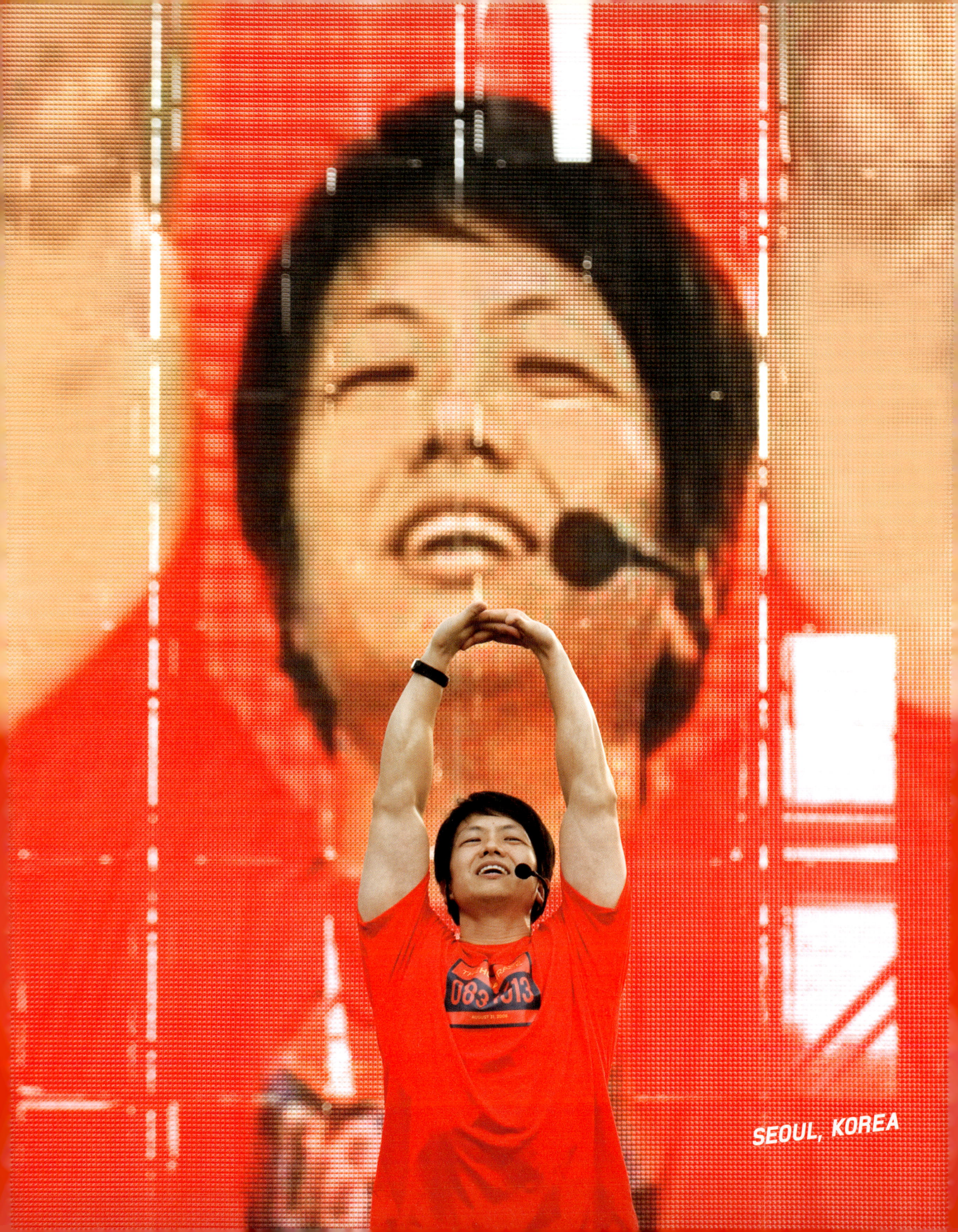
SEOUL, KOREA

VINCENTE FURGIUELE
RESTAURANT OWNER
LIMA, PERU

Vincente Furgiuele, 54, was born in Argentina, but has lived in Peru since he was 9. He owns a seafood restaurant, Canta Rana (the Singing Frog), that is popular with runners and other athletes. The walls are decorated with autographed posters, photographs and athletic medals, reflecting his passion for soccer, running and other sports. "I love space and freedom and I'm hyperactive, so running brings all that together in a positive way. If there's a day when I can't run, I feel I started the day wrong. I had a heart condition last year, so I had to spend some time in the hospital and had antibiotics pumped into me for more than a month. I think the fact that I'm a runner saved my life, because it helped me maintain a positive attitude. Running has created a sort of family in my life and my greatest friends are those who run with me. And when I have sentimental problems—like, for example, if I break up with my girlfriend—my running friends save me from my grief.

"A good friend of mine is always competing against me on our runs, but for The Human Race, he said, 'Today we will run together.' I think this was the most beautiful of all the Nike races in Lima because of the people, the sunshine in the middle of winter and the magic that came from this combination."

SELCUK KOCUM
BELGRADE FOREST RUNNING GROUP
ISTANBUL, TURKEY

Selcuk (far left) has run with a group in the Belgrade Forest since 1999. "Running is difficult in Istanbul—traffic is terrible and it's hard to meet friends after work. So we meet in the forest on weekends; it's both an escape and a place to see the people I really want to see.

"The first time I ran a marathon, we crossed the Bosporus Bridge at six kilometers. My friend has a house close by, so we decided to stop and have breakfast instead of finishing. My second marathon, same thing: At 6K we decided, 'Eh, that's enough,' and had breakfast again. But for The Human Race, I was determined: no breakfast. I feel very lucky to have run it. Sharing this excitement with the whole world made me feel good. We all did a good thing together."

JOE CONSTANTY
ENTREPRENEUR
SHANGHAI, CHINA

"I run to explore a city—whichever city I happen to be in. It's slower than driving around in a car, but so much more captivating. I'm surprised every single day by what I find when I hit the streets.

"I took up running seriously about two years ago. Last May, I was pounding the streets at 7:45 A.M. to avoid rush hour, with rap music blasting through my MP3 player. Without any warning, a car smashed into my right knee, spun me around, then crashed into my left leg and sent me soaring. My collarbone was shattered, but apart from that, there was no major damage. Five months after the accident, I was competing again, and running in The Human Race is proof that I've made a full recovery. (Not to sound preachy, but needless to say, I never train on the streets anymore with my earbuds in.)

"The Human Race was the best organized race I've run in China, hands down. The sight of thousands of people running together in red shirts was awesome. There were so many runners that I was crossing the finishing line as some people were barely starting!"

WILLIAM KOLONG PIOTH
"LOST BOYS OF SUDAN"
UNHCR, THE UN REFUGEE AGENCY'S
NINEMILLION.ORG CAMPAIGN
VANCOUVER, CANADA

In hindsight, William Kolong Pioth realizes that he might not have trained long enough for The Nike+ Human Race. A handyman who oversees building facilities at a large mall in Vancouver, Pioth isn't a longtime runner but has always been athletic. To prepare for this special 10K, though, he says he "trained like crazy" by doing 12 daily laps of a nearby soccer field. After finishing The Nike+ Human Race, though, he knows he didn't run enough laps. "It was a little hard for me," he says, "but I made it. The thing is, you run, run, run, and you think you're almost there, and then you look up and see you're just at the 3K mark."

Pioth has handled many tougher situations in his life. He's a "Lost Boy," one of the thousands of children who escaped war-torn Sudan and survived years in UNHCR refugee camps before relocating to North America. Pioth has harrowing tales of a three-month forced march east into Ethiopia at the age of 9—he and the others were shepherded by soldiers; friends were lost in the jungle, eaten by lions, starved or drowned jumping into rivers to escape. He survived, but he knows that tens of thousands of Sudanese didn't make it out.

Now 32 and a Canadian citizen, Pioth is one of the leaders in an immigrant group called the South Sudanese of B.C. Association. Among his many other responsibilities, he directs a tutoring and literacy network called Homework, which helps kids who now find themselves 8,000 miles from their homeland.

For The Nike+ Human Race, Pioth ran with seven other Lost Boys including Kalahan Deng (right and below, with family), along with 20 other Sudanese refugees from the Vancouver area. Another carload of Sudanese drove up from Tacoma, Washington, to run with them. Still others came out just to support the runners. "I wasn't sure I could make 10K, but I wanted to try," Pioth says. "We are not real runners, we did it for fun."

He says The Nike+ Human Race gave a boost to his community, raising funds for three international causes (including refugees). "To someone like me who grew up in these camps, sports and education were one of the things that kept us together. On race day, a lot of people in our community showed up, and we met new people. Everybody on our team is really into running now, and we pledge to train to be ready to do another race again next year. This was a really good moment for us."

MELANIE ANGEL
JOURNALIST
LONDON, ENGLAND

"I feel much worse than most people do after a race—I'm nauseated, dizzy and my blood pressure drops. After the last marathon in London, I spent two hours in the medical tent. After New York, I got an IV and was sent to the hospital. I question my sanity and think I shouldn't do marathons, but pain goes with running. I'm 51 and didn't run my first race until I was 40. A chance dinner party conversation led to me running a half-marathon. The Human Race had a special meaning for me: My daughter left for a year in Israel that night, so I was emotional, but running clears my head. I get peace of mind from it."

OSCAR RUÍZ
ARMY MAJOR
BOGOTÁ, COLOMBIA

"My accident took place in June 2007. I was a counterguerrilla battalion commander and I stepped on a land mine in San Vicente del Caguán. My left foot was gone, but thank God the skies were clear, so my men were able to call in a helicopter and get me out of there fast. The first day I was in shock: the pain, the amputation, everybody worrying about me. I got used to saying, 'I'm fine; my brain is working perfectly, I have my eyes, my ears, my hands. I've lost a foot, but I can get a substitute for that.' But I woke up many mornings asking myself, 'What's going to happen to me?' I was a soldier fighting in a war, and now what? Our Army's top general visited me and said: 'You have to go on.'

"I spent 20 days in the military hospital and then started my rehabilitation. It was hard, but I couldn't allow myself to be weak. The natural impulse is to blame everything bad that happens to you on the accident, but you cannot let that happen.

"Around that time the commander of the Presidential Battalion told me they were training for a Nike 10K, so I decided to take it as my first challenge. I told my former Colonel, 'I want to run in the race. Well, not run—I'm going to walk.' I didn't even have the prosthesis yet—I didn't get it until 15 days before the race.

"The race was spectacular—all those people, all that energy. My wife walked with me. I had to get used to the prosthesis; it hurt a little, but I was able to deal with it. When I was getting close to the finish line, the Presidential Battalion was waiting for me, other people were clapping and shouting, 'You can do it!' And, yes, I could. I finished in one hour and 49 minutes. There were about 3,000 people who finished behind me—that's motivating! That race proved to me that this accident is not an obstacle, that I can achieve my goals.

"My wife and I have now run three races, one of them a half-marathon. I can run three kilometers without a problem. After that I have to stop, take the prosthesis off, wash the sweat away, put it back on. Then I walk about one kilometer and then run some more. My wife and two daughters are running The Human Race with me, and my goal is to finish in one hour. I'm going to run a Nike race every year. It's a special event for me, because that first race was my initial step on a very long road."

U.S. AIR FORCE
LOS ANGELES, CALIFORNIA

The flexibility of The Nike+ Human Race, which encouraged participants to make a virtual run if they couldn't make it to one of the official events, allowed runners at the Los Angeles Air Force Base in El Segundo, a suburb of Los Angeles, to run together, albeit alone.

Members of the base's 12-member marathon team had hoped to run en masse; however, as August 31 drew closer, they realized their schedules would not permit it. So they went their own ways but still found a way to run as one. Lt. Col. Donald Wilson, the team's alternate, had already

committed to taking his daughter to run her first half-marathon that day. They ran in her event, and submitted their 10K times for The Nike+ Human Race.

Capt. David Wisniewski, an engineer and program manager, knew he would be in San Francisco the night of the race, so he ran there. "I treated it like a Sunday afternoon jog," he says, "and added five miles—a piece-of-cake distance for a marathoner."

Lt. Amanda Devuono, a nautical engineer who has run since high school, plotted out a 10K course in her neighborhood and ran by herself. "It was cool, because I knew I was one of so many people out there doing this," she says. "Usually when you race, you're running against the clock. This was different because we all knew how many other people were involved."

PAUL TERGAT
WORLD CHAMPION RUNNER
ROME, ITALY

"Growing up in Kenya's Rift Valley, I never knew I had any special talent. My father was a traditional African of the Tugen tribe, with three wives, and I lived in a one-room mud hut with my mother and three of my 17 siblings. We didn't have much in the way of food—sometimes one meal a day was a luxury. When I was 7, the United Nations World Food Programme started a program in my village. We children wanted to be in school because there was a hot lunch—some of my friends walked 10 kilometers to get there.

"I didn't start running until I joined the Air Force; I've now won five consecutive world championships in cross-country, and set world records for the 10K, the half-marathon and the marathon.

"Since 2004, I've been an Ambassador Against Hunger for the UN World Food Programme—the people who gave me an opportunity when I was a kid. I've witnessed incredible suffering in Darfur, Somalia and the northern corridor of Kenya traveling with WFP. I also started my own foundation to give disadvantaged young athletes a chance.

"I'm 39 but I'm not finished with running. It's my passion, and nobody is going to take it from me. I couldn't train this year because I got recalled to the Kenyan Air Force for four months, after post-election violence in our country, but I'm ready to get back to competing. In The Human Race, everybody was a winner, regardless of their times, because we were all running for humanity."

CATHERINE PLUME
WWF
RAN IN U.S. NATIONAL ARBORETUM

As forest director for field programs and the leader of WWF's work in Chile, Catherine Plume dabbles in forestry, salmon fisheries, and the conservation of blue whales. "If I want to take full advantage of the opportunities my work presents me," she says, "I have to stay in shape."

As a kid, she loved the outdoors. "The creek behind our house was our playground, and we spent hours back there having all sorts of adventures." She studied forestry at a small university in East Texas, but didn't know what to do with her degree, so she became a Peace Corps volunteer, flew to Paraguay and helped start a tree nursery. "That launched my career in conservation. When I returned to Paraguay 10 years later, the nursery was still there. It was really moving." Cathy has also lived in Togo, Mali and Bolivia. "It's great to work for WWF because it has a global presence. If we're dealing with a business in Chile that's not willing to make some positive environmental change, we can pressure them by talking to buyers of their products in another country. We have access to a lot of pressure points. WWF is very powerful."

One of her favorite moments came in Bolivia. Farmers were building terraces to stop erosion in a cornfield. Cathy and some staff offered to pitch in. "These guys didn't know what to do with a woman who wanted to help out, but they played along. Not long after we'd started to work, they suggested that we break." Unfortunately for Cathy, a huge festival had ended just a few days before, so the farmers had some local brew—chicha—left over. Since Cathy was the guest, she was offered the first chug from a communal gourd. "It looked disgusting," she says. "Flies were floating in the milky liquid, which was sour and spoiled. It was the last thing I wanted to drink. In Bolivian custom, drinks are served to Mother Earth—Pacha Mama—by spilling some on the ground. I figured Pacha Mama was going to be my savior, so I started giving her a lot of my chicha." Finally, one of the farmers called her out—"Señorita, you don't have to give Pacha Mama so much!" This experience reinforced for Cathy the importance of establishing local relationships.

Cathy ran occasionally in college, but only picked up the sport again two years ago. "Most of the time I wonder why I'm beating up my body," she says, "but every once in a while, everything is just right and I have an amazing run that really makes me feel good."

When Nike joined Climate Savers in 2001, it set an ambitious target of reducing greenhouse gas emissions by 13 percent from Nike-owned operations and business travel from 1998 levels. Nike is achieving these reductions and developing a plan to curb emissions throughout the supply chain. "Nike is a trusted partner with WWF, and we think mobilizing runners to help highlight our climate change efforts globally is fantastic," Cathy says. "The Human Race was a chance to bring people around the world into the fight against climate change and protect some of the most biodiverse places on Earth."

JOSÉ JUAN PELAEZ MIRANDA
RUNNER
LIMA, PERU

José Juan Pelaez Miranda, who is 81 years old, was born in Lima and has spent all his life there. He has run in three Nike 10Ks, and is proud to say that he was never the last person to finish. He loves running for many reasons, but most of all because, he says, "it is a great way to meet people, and to share their passion."

"I run in a group that sets out at 5 A.M. The streets are full of long shadows from the rising sun, and it's cool in the summer. It's beautifully calm—not a soul to be seen. These are beautiful moments that other people miss because they're asleep. When we finish, some people are just starting their day, while others are just finishing the day before. A person may come to run with us directly from a party, only stopping at home to change.

"After my husband and I finished The Human Race, we ran the route again. The first 10K was for fun, the second 10K was training."

EMILSE LORENA CIEZAR
RUNNER IN DISGUISE
BUENOS AIRES, ARGENTINA

"In June of 1999, my tibia was smashed into bits in an accident and my fibula practically disappeared. I was bedridden for four months and had a really tough rehab. Even today, I have 12 pretty screws holding a plate in my leg. As a consequence, I gained weight, eating my way up to 254 pounds.

"I started spinning and doing other exercises, and as soon as I lost enough weight, I started to run again. The strength to do this had to come from within. There are no magic recipes. Since I started running again in 2004, I've completed more than 114 road and adventure races.

"The idea of running in a costume came from my passion for running. I always make it an elaborate production that I put a lot of time and energy into. The idea is to go with a distinct 'look' for each race and to pass on my good feelings to others. During a 10K last year, I carried two skulls in my hands, with skulls painted on my face. I also wore a long purple wig."

ROBINSON VIVOR
COMPETITIVE RACE WALKER
QUITO, ECUADOR

Ecuador's sole claim to big international competition has been in race-walking, a sport that requires the athlete to have one foot touching the ground at all times. Jefferson Pérez won the country's first-ever gold medal in 1996 in the 20K event and went on to win three straight world championships and a silver medal in Beijing. His example has inspired other Ecuadorans. One of his most promising devotees is Robinson Vivor, 21. "I was 10 when Jefferson won his first medal," he says. "That's what got me into track and field." Vivor won a race-walking silver in the Juvenile Pan American Games in 2005, but a string of injuries put him out of elite racing this year. You wouldn't know he was injured if you saw him strenuously walking alongside runners in training for The Nike+ Human Race. Though his sport emphasizes muscle groups different from those used in running, he ran in The Nike+ Human Race. "Running is more effortless, more natural," he says. "But it's a great complement to race-walking while I get back into form."

MARIEL VIDAL
PHOTOGRAPHER
MADRID, SPAIN

Mariel Vidal has been running since her boyfriend introduced her to the sport when she was 18. She, in turn, inspired her sister, Chari, to take it up as well. "I've lived in a lot of different countries, but I always take my running shoes with me," Mariel says. For the past 17 years, ever since she met her Spanish husband, her home has been Toledo, Spain.

Ten thousand kilometers away, Chari prefers the noise and crowds of Lima, Peru, and for the past five years, she has been running with a group called Peru Runners. "I used to get bored when I ran by myself," she says. "But now I'm part of this big group, and it's great—running makes me feel like I'm entering a different dimension."

CHARI VIDAL
EVENTS COORDINATOR, "PERU RUNNERS" LIMA, PERU

When the sisters visit each other, they like to run together, but The Nike+ Human Race offered them a chance to do that without either of them having to pack a suitcase. "As soon as I heard about the race, I thought how lovely it would be to share the race with Chari," says Mariel, "even if it was only virtually." After the race, Chari said, "I enjoyed the race, the route, the music, everything. I was worried about how Mariel would do, though, because it's winter here, but it's summer in Madrid and really hot."

"I was thinking about Chari the whole time I was running," says Mariel, "and when we spoke later, we realized we had similar experiences. It was very moving for both of us to be united with all of those people in a single cause. Imagine what we could do if the whole world got together to run."

"We are friends and co-workers in El Paso," explains Amanda. "We knew that we wanted to run The Human Race, but felt that since it's a global event we should head out somewhere random and different. We decided to come to Seoul because it is about as far away from Texas as we could have gone. We had an incredible time, as well as some interesting meals. We ate something slippery last night and I still don't know what it was."

SULEIMAN RIFAI
BLIND RUNNER
NEW YORK, NEW YORK

"I jumped into the air when I crossed the finish line of The Human Race, but that wasn't unusual. I always jump at the end of races, because every time I finish it feels like magic. I am grateful to be outside hearing the birds, feeling the warm sun or moist raindrops, and moving worry-free because I know my guide, to whom I am tethered by a string, won't let me bump into scaffolding or fall into a pothole.

"I was born in 1960 in Dar es Salaam. At 14, I was diagnosed with retinitis pigmentosa; the doctor said I would eventually go blind. The diagnosis felt like a death sentence. I rarely left the house and was a loner. When I was 19, my youngest sister invited me to live with her in New York City, and arranged for me to get training at Lighthouse International, a center for visually impaired people. Finally, I had hope. The staff there taught me to use a cane, to take the bus and subway, and to read Braille. Best of all, I made friends for the first time in eons and felt like I had a life. I earned a bachelor's degree in social work in 1997 and a master's in 1998. But getting a job wasn't easy. I had lots of interviews, but when prospective employers saw my cane, they aways got nervous. After several months, though, a center for homeless women in Brooklyn hired me. Three years later, I got a job counseling disabled people in Manhattan.

"My life took another major turn in 2003 when I met Rick Lipsey on the subway. He told me about Achilles, a track club for disabled people, and invited me to a workout in Central Park. I can still picture that first run. I hadn't run since I was a little boy, but I felt at home because of the camaraderie. Also, I wanted to win. 'We're not racing,' Rick said. 'Oh, but I want to go fast,' I replied. 'Maybe I will be the best runner.' We ran four miles that day, but I could have run forever. Two years later, I completed my first marathon, and now I do New York every year.

"With Rick's help, I've also taken up golf, cross-country skiing and swimming. People often ask how a blind person can do such things. I can only say that I don't see limitations, just opportunities. I know what it's like to wallow in self-pity, and I will never let myself go down that road again. I want to embrace the challenges that come each day. That's why I was eager to experience The Human Race. The course was very narrow and winding, along mostly dirt paths, but with the help of my wonderful guides, I ran my heart out and did well. I didn't win, but maybe I will next time. And when I do, I'll jump for joy."

HECTOR FARTO
RUNNING CONVERT
SÃO PAOLO, BRAZIL

Hector Farto was your typical party-hearty 20-something: He worked late as a bartender, went to bed when the sun was rising and woke up when it was setting. He smoked too much, drank too much and ate too much junk food. Exercise? Just the occasional "cheat run" once a week, but that was more to flirt with girls at the park than for the exercise. All that changed last summer when he was selected to take part in Nike's 30-day Challenge. He was closely monitored by a coach, a doctor and a physiotherapist. The goal was to see how many kilometers he could run in 30 days.

Hector says he was plagued by knee pains, tiredness, laziness and a relentless coach, but he learned to eat properly, go to bed at a reasonable time and cut down on the partying. At the end of the 30 days, he had run almost 320 kilometers. He now swears that he'll never give up running—he even quit his bartending job and started working as a graphic designer. Farto says he felt exhilarated crossing the finish line for The Nike+ Human Race. When asked what has changed in his life, he laughed and answered, "Everything."

DARLA BRIGGS
THREE GENERATIONS
VANCOUVER, CANADA

"My mother is way more of a runner than I ever was. She's a breast-cancer survivor, and she runs for breast cancer and other causes. When I found out about The Human Race, my mother and I decided to run together, and push my daughter in a runner's stroller so that we'd have three generations of women in the race. And it was fabulous! We did it in about an hour and five minutes. My mom and I took turns pushing the stroller. Sometimes we both had one hand on it and pushed it together. Everyone in the race was really positive and encouraging. At one point, I said to my mom, 'Wow, you are running really fast.' She replied, 'I'm just trying to keep up with you!' I said, 'I was trying to keep up with you!' So we agreed to pace ourselves until the last two kilometers, and then we gave it our all. We are still arguing over which of us is more proud of the other!"

"On April 4, 2007, in the early morning hours the day after my 32nd birthday, I felt a rush of pain shoot through my left arm and then my chest. I immediately went to the nearest clinic, where I was treated for a heart attack. My lifestyle was to blame—heavy smoking, working long hours, too much stress and no exercise. The doctors told me to stop smoking and get plenty of physical activity. At first, all I could do was walk for 20 minutes. Today, after months of training five or six days a week, with an average of 30 or more miles per week, the possibilities are endless. I am in the best shape of my life. This morning I ran 10 easy miles in under 1:35:00. I would have never thought it possible, but with hard work, incredible coaching, the support of fellow runners and, most important, the love of my family—I have changed my life. That is why I run: for my wife and my three beautiful boys."

CHRIS PREST
PRODUCT DESIGN ENGINEER, CANCER SURVIVOR
AUSTIN, TEXAS

"My girlfriend was the one who suggested I go to the doctor. In March, a suspicious lump on my left testicle had, ahem, aroused some concern, but I did the typical guy thing and dismissed it—I was due to fly to China the next morning for business. Fortunately, common sense prevailed, and we decided to go to the emergency room. The initial test was an ultrasound, to inspect the lump. Then they did blood work, which showed I had highly elevated tumor marker scores. The doctors said I needed immediate surgery, because the tumor was so large and one of my marker scores was over 28,000—you have cancer if the score is over six!

"The next day, I had the bollock chopped off. The tumor was sent away for analysis, and the pathology results told us the cancer was in my bloodstream. The doctors did further tests, which showed it might have spread to lymph nodes in my abdomen. A month after my first operation, they opened up my abdomen and removed them. The pathology results for this operation came back clean, and we thought the cancer was gone.

"A month later, I had a routine checkup and my doctors found indications of cancer. I started chemo the next day. All I could do was research the crap out of the disease and possible treatments so that I could discuss my options intelligently with my doctors. I realized that there were very few things that I could do to improve my odds, but I made sure that I did every one of them—things like staying out of crowds when my immune system was down, and making sure that I didn't flinch when the nurses were trying to inject me with chemo so that they were less likely to miss my vein.

"There are few times in life when you feel almost completely helpless—the things that I was doing to help myself seemed like such insignificant acts. That is why I consider my cancer experience a positive one: Now that I'm cancer-free (at least for now), I feel so empowered. I have complete control over my health. Before I was focusing too much on work; now I make sure I work out regularly. When the third round of chemo ended in July, I hit the gym.

"For many people The Human Race is the culmination of weeks or even months of training. For me it's the start of a new chapter of my life, in which I am in control of my destiny. For a while I couldn't decide how I was going to approach the race—run it hard or ease up and run it with my girlfriend. In the end, we decided to run together. She's been supportive throughout all this, so it was my turn to return the favor and stick by her side."

RUNNING FOR A CAUSE

The first human ever to run for a cause may have been a caveman fleeing a saber-toothed tiger. He wasn't looking to save mankind. Just himself.

In mankind's earliest recorded history, the superstar of the running world was Pheidippides, the original marathoner. In 490 B.C., when the Persians invaded Athens, Pheidippides was dispatched to seek military aid from the Spartans—140 miles away. Despite the distance, we are told that our hero ran to Sparta like a "fire" through a field of "stubble." Alas, the Spartans weren't interested, so he ran the 140 miles back to Athens.

The story goes that en route the herald met Pan, the goat god, who promised to support the Athenians. When the Persians were subsequently routed on the plains of Marathon, Pheidippides ran 26 miles to Athens with news of the Greek victory. He thereby gave chilling resonance to the term "finishing line" by promptly dropping dead.

Ever since then, running has been used to advance causes. In 2000 in Sydney, an athlete of Aboriginal descent won the women's 400-meter race in driving rain. She then set off around the track with Aboriginal and Australian flags entwined to address the race issue and, she said later, to acknowledge "Aboriginal pain."

The universal popularity of running makes it a valuable marketing and fund-raising tool for a range of civic groups, environmentalists and charities; some have even created professionally trained track teams that consist entirely of donors. They compete in road races throughout the country.

Individual runners have competed to stop drug abuse and end famine in Ethiopia, to save hospitals and protect wildlife, to raise money for everything from aid for injured war veterans to marching band instruments.

Here is a timeline of some of the great "cause" runs that have been held over the last three decades:

1980: A Canadian who lost a leg to osteosarcoma, set out to run from Newfoundland to British Columbia with one prosthetic leg; his goal was to raise money for cancer research. His "Marathon of Hope" ended after 143 days and 3,339 miles because his bone cancer had spread to his lungs. The runner became a national hero; his death in 1981 inspired an annual run.

1981: A Kentucky marathoner ran 146 miles in 36 hours to promote the work of the American Lung Association.

1983: The inaugural Susan B. Komen Race for the Cure was held in Dallas, with 800 participants. In the ensuing years, the 5K run, which benefits breast cancer research, has grown to a global series of nearly 120 races with more than 1.5 million participants.

1998: Four members of World T.E.A.M. Sports, a squad of able-bodied and handicapped runners, ran 150 miles across the Sahara desert in six days. One runner had lost a leg after stepping on a mine in Vietnam; another was blind.

2007: The 106 Canadians who competed in an Athens marathon raised some $670,000 for the Arthritis Society.

And in 2008, of course, The Nike+ Human Race.

In most of these races, runners put aside a little self-absorption, and dashed to do good. American road races and walks such as The Nike+ Human Race now generate a billion dollars every year for charity and research. The hefty entry fees mean that running is the only sport in which the slowest pay through the nose for the privilege of being beaten by the fastest—and can feel good about themselves, no matter where they finish.

—Franz Lidz,
Award-Winning Sports Journalist

FOOT POWER

THE RAW ENERGY PRODUCED BY THE NIKE+ HUMAN RACE IN CALORIES BURNED BY RUNNERS IS EQUIVALENT TO USING THESE AMOUNTS OF TRADITIONAL POWER SOURCES:

**779,225 runners x 10K = 647,535,975 calories
= 2.70929052 x 10⁹ joules**

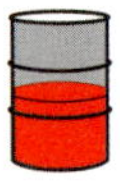

→ .444 barrels of oil

→ .033 grams of Uranium

→ 169.33 pounds of coal

→ 289,454 AA batteries × 1000

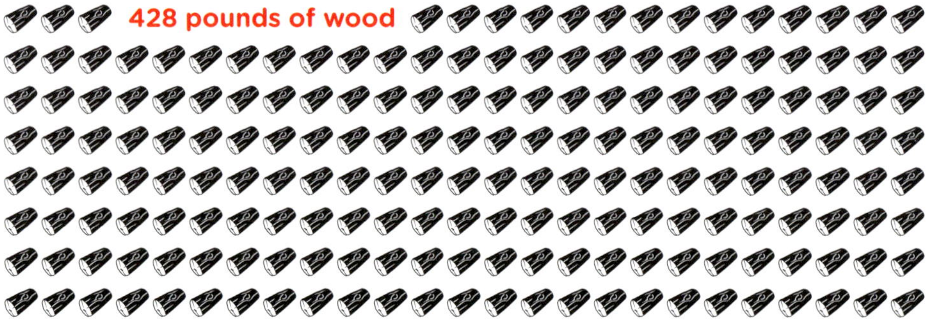

→ 428 pounds of wood × 2

→ ← 350,575 miles • 350,575 miles →

Imagine the black dot to the left is centered in a circle whose edges are 350,575 miles in all directions. This ratio represents the amount of energy burned by all the runners in The Nike+ Human Race as a fraction of the total energy released by the sun every second.

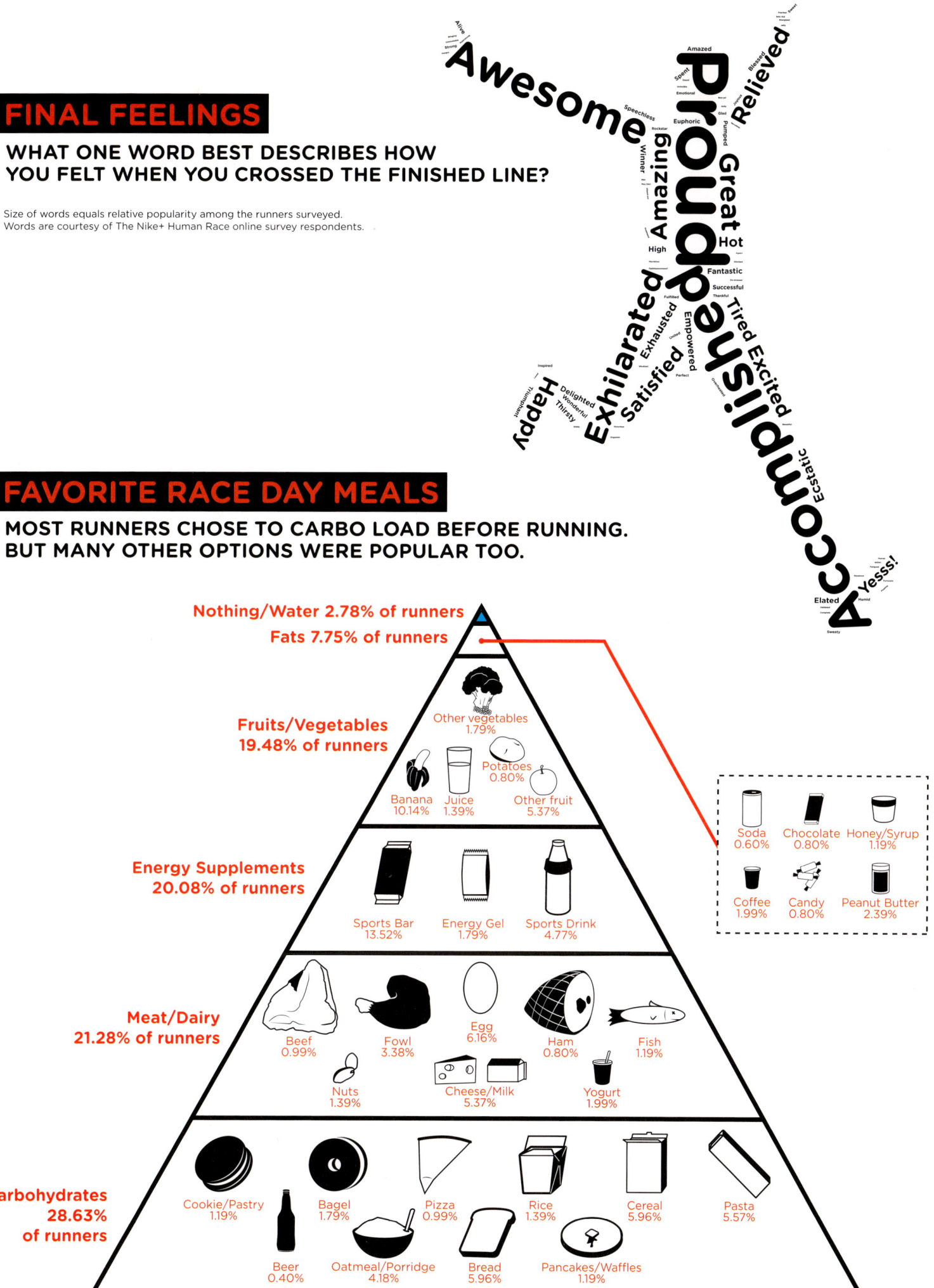

ITIR ERHART
FOUNDER OF ADIM ADIM (STEP BY STEP) ISTANBUL, TURKEY

"In the U.S. I ran with a group which raised money for leukemia patients. Finishing a marathon feels great, but doing something good with it feels even better. When I moved back to Turkey, I said, 'Why don't we bring that model here?' We decided to run for an organization that gives better wheelchairs to paraplegics. One reason we chose that group was that we can run, and these people can't even move. We called our charity Adim Adim, which means "step by step." By running, we make it possible for them to move.

"I would like to see more people running in Turkey. I met many people excited about The Human Race who weren't even serious runners; and after this race, I think they will run again. My favorite moment from that day was running over the Bosporus Bridge—against an indigo sky, with the monuments lit on the shore, the sound of the boats, the smell of the sea and the thousands of runners pausing to admire this magical scene. That will be forever engraved in my memory."

MANAL CHOURAFA
FIRST 10K
PARIS, FRANCE

"I've only been running for four months. One day, my karate instructor told me I had to run between our training sessions, so I gave it a go. I ran once a week in the beginning, but after watching my brother-in-law get up at 4:30 A.M. every day for six months to train for a triathlon, I figured I could at least run every other day. So I ran more, and I'm still running. But 10K was a challenge for me. My usual route is 5.4 kilometers, and I struggle every time. But The Human Race brought everything to a whole different level. The cool thing was that on race day, I wasn't doing it alone. I ran for all the people I've met during my travels around the world as a nurse in India, the Middle East, Africa, and for my childhood friends in Jordan."

FELICIA HARDEN-BRADFORD, VALERIE VIRAMONTES AND CHRISTINE GARRISON
"MOCHA MOMS"
NEW YORK, NEW YORK

We're in Harlem, the corner of 125th Street and Lexington Avenue. Three African-American mothers wearing red shirts and black sweats look at the long line of people waiting for the shuttle to take them to Randall's Island for The Nike+ Human Race in New York City and quickly decide to hail a cab instead. They want some quiet so that they can gather their emotions after a long week of child rearing, cooking and tending to the sick. Also, one of their own has died—Bernadette lost her husband the day before. He was just 33 when he succumbed to stomach and lung cancer only weeks after being diagnosed. Felicia Harden-Bradford, Valerie Viramontes and Christine Garrison are running The Nike+ Human Race for Bernadette, and the memory of her husband.

The women have bonded through Mocha Moms, a support group for stay-at-home mothers of color. "I don't think black women exercise as much as we should because of so many competing priorities in our lives," Harden-Bradford says. "Often, black women are the heads of their household, without the help of a significant other. So when I see another black chick exercising, I make a point of smiling and giving her the 'You go, girl!' look."

After haggling over the fare with their cabbie and then navigating through a sea of thousands of runners, the women finally make it to the starting line, where they bow their heads to pray for Bernadette's family. Starting near the back, they struggle to find their pace on the crowded course. At the three-mile mark, a spectator yells to Harden-Bradford, "Go ahead, Afro girl!"

Viramontes arrived here this morning after a 10-hour waitressing shift. "You've already run 10 miles today around this restaurant," a co-worker told her as she walked out the door. Garrison came from a full day of church activities with her preacher husband. "Thank God for the running stations on the course," she said afterward. "I needed every one of them."

At dusk, the three women finish their first 10K. "I feel proud," says Viramontes. "We all have children. We're fit. We're strong black women." She smiles. "I feel like having sex. I haven't felt like having sex in a long time."

Over a post-race yogurt parfait, looking forward to baths and bedtime, they discuss how to get more mothers involved in their next race, a half-marathon in January, and Harden-Bradford sums up the Mocha Mom philosophy: "We will run longer and faster—together."

"I RUN TO KEEP MY SANITY. I RUN TO EAT WHAT I WANT. I RUN BECAUSE I CAN. THE HUMAN RACE WAS MY FIRST 10K; IN FACT, IT WAS MY FIRST RACE OF ANY KIND! I TURNED 40 THIS YEAR AND NEEDED TO PROVE TO MYSELF THAT 40 REALLY IS THE NEW 25. AND I DID. AND I FEEL REALLY, REALLY GOOD ABOUT MYSELF. I RAN PAST PEOPLE 20 YEARS YOUNGER THAN ME. I EVEN SPRINTED THE LAST KILOMETER! HERE'S TO HOPING THAT THAT FINAL SPRINT IS A METAPHOR FOR MY LIFE—THAT THE BEST IS YET TO COME!"
—MARY KATHRYN HALL
SCHERTZ, TEXAS

"I ABSOLUTELY HATED RUNNING. I COULDN'T DO IT AND I DIDN'T UNDERSTAND IT. BUT WHEN I GRADUATED FROM COLLEGE, I REALIZED I HAD PUT ON THE FRESHMAN 15, PLUS THE SOPHOMORE 12, THE JUNIOR 13 AND THE SENIOR 20. MY DOCTOR TOLD ME THAT I HAD DEVELOPED GERD DUE TO THE EXCESS WEIGHT. SO I TOOK UP RUNNING. ONCE I LEARNED HOW TO RUN, I BEGAN TO LOVE IT. NOW, AFTER A FEW MONTHS OF TRAINING, I'M RUNNING WITH MY BOYFRIEND AND FRIENDS IN THE HUMAN RACE. I'M DOING IT NOT ONLY TO BECOME PART OF HISTORY BUT TO PROVE TO MYSELF THAT I CAN DO ANYTHING I PUT MY MIND TO. I WILL FINISH THIS RACE. YOU CAN BE YOUR GREATEST CHEERLEADER OR YOUR BIGGEST FOE. IT'S YOUR CHOICE."
—LAUREN SHAPIRO
MONROE, NEW JERSEY

"I RUN THIS DISTANCE VERY OFTEN, BUT I DO IT QUITE SLOWLY, JUST TO GET MYSELF MOVING. KNOWING THAT SO MANY WOULD RUN IT TOGETHER IN THE HUMAN RACE, AND FOR CHARITY, MADE IT SPECIAL FOR ME. AND MY RESULTS SHOWED THIS: I BROKE MY MILE, 5K AND 10K RECORDS AFTER ALMOST A YEAR!"
—DANIJEL BRENER
BUDAPEST, HUNGARY

"I SPENT MOST OF MY LIFE IN PERU WITH MY HUSBAND AND CHILDREN. BACK THEN RUNNING WAS MY ONLY SPORT. BUT AFTER FINISHING A MARATHON IN 1985, I GOT A SERIOUS KNEE INJURY AND HAD TO SWITCH TO OTHER SPORTS. IN 2005, I MOVED TO SOUTHEAST ASIA WITH MY HUSBAND. TWO MONTHS AGO MY SON, WHO STAYED IN PERU, TOLD US THAT HE HAD REGISTERED FOR THE HUMAN RACE IN LIMA AND CONVINCED US TO RUN IT IN SINGAPORE. I WAS IMMEDIATELY SEDUCED BY THE IDEA OF 'SHARING' THE RACE WITH HIM. MY BEST MEMORY IS WHEN I GOT TO THE SEVENTH KILOMETER, WHEN NOT ONLY MY KNEE BUT MY ANKLES AND THIGHS WERE BEGGING ME TO STOP AND I ANSWERED, 'NO WAY!' WITH A SMILE. I FELT THAT MY SON WAS—SOMEHOW—AT MY SIDE, SUPPORTING ME, URGING ME TO KEEP RUNNING."
—LYDIA ECHEVERRIA
SINGAPORE

"I RAN AS PART OF MY HUSBAND'S WEDDING GIFT. WE TRAINED FOR THREE MONTHS (EVEN THROUGH THE CHAOS OF PLANNING OUR WEDDING!), THEN FLEW TO CHICAGO JUST TO RUN IN THE HUMAN RACE. IT WAS OUR FIRST TRIP AS A MARRIED COUPLE AND OUR FIRST RACE TOGETHER. IT WAS THE MOST INCREDIBLE THING I HAVE EVER BEEN A PART OF."
—ANJI PAUMIER
GASTONIA, NORTH CAROLINA

"I'M NOT A NATURAL RUNNER, BUT I COULDN'T PASS UP THE CHANCE TO BE PART OF A WORLDWIDE RACE AND TO START FROM THE ICONIC WEMBLEY STADIUM. AND NOW, THE DAY AFTER THE HUMAN RACE, I AM HOOKED. DESPITE A TORRENTIAL DOWNPOUR, THE ATMOSPHERE WAS ELECTRIC: THE STEWARDS, SUPPORTERS AND OTHER RUNNERS SHOUTING ENCOURAGEMENT GAVE ME GOOSE BUMPS! NOW ALL I CAN THINK ABOUT IS WHEN I CAN RUN AGAIN AND FEEL THAT BUZZ. (AND WHEN WILL I STOP ACHING?!)"
—STEPHANIE BAYLISS
REDDITCH, ENGLAND

JULIEN SORBON
RUNNING WITH HIS FATHER
PARIS, FRANCE

"Sports have been my dad's great passion forever, and he passed that passion on to me at an early age. As soon as I could walk, he had me learning to ride a bike, and every weekend he brought me to the park to run myself silly. He was always there for me when it came to my different competitions. Whether it was soccer—still my main sport—or track or basketball or judo, he drove me to every practice, he was at every match. He still comes when I have a match with my local soccer team. And now we have teamed up for The Human Race. It was the first time we ran a race together. As we've gotten older, we've shared fewer moments together, but this race makes for a great memory for both of us."

VLADIMIR GUERRA
FOUNDER, "SILVIO'S RUNNERS" QUITO, ECUADOR

Years ago, four-time world marathon champion Silvio Guerra organized a running club for some of Quito's mechanics, masons and cleaning women; some of the members even shine shoes for a living. The most prominent runner to emerge from this pack is Franklin Tenorio, who ran the marathon in Beijing. Silvio's brother Vladimir, who's also a top distance runner, trains the group four mornings a week. These so-called odd-jobbers are highly motivated and are always looking for a race. A number of them ran Quito's church run on August 30 and The Nike+ Human Race the next day. Although they have less time to train than many of the top runners they compete against, Guerra predicted his runners would place in the top three in their age groups for The Nike+ Human Race.

Guerra is a good runner and a better prognosticator—he finished first in Quito's Nike+ Human Race. "I felt really good from the beginning, but my largest trophy is with me today—my daughter, Annie. On the 15th of October she will be 1 year old."

"My wife died 12 years ago. I live alone and have no children. I fill my time with two hobbies: reading and athletics. I swim or jog every other day. It's a way to feed my body and spirit. If you don't keep moving, you deteriorate and you die.

"These days, everything is so technology-based. Kids are always on their cell phones or on the Internet instead of getting outside and exercising. We don't take care of our bodies, and that's so essential to having a good, long life.

"Dr. José Ghergo organized a group of retirees: I'm 95, Osvaldo is 86, Santiago is 76 and the other Horacio is 74. Dr. Ghergo named us Carbon 14, for the element used to date fossils. We compete in races as a relay team about two or three times a year, and we share a special camaraderie.

"I ran in a 7K in 2006 that finished in the River Plate soccer stadium; when I entered it, thousands of people applauded me and that felt amazing. It filled me with so much emotion that I cried. My dream is to set a world record, to do something amazing for someone my age. Not many people reach my age, and even fewer do what I can do.

"The Human Race was one of the most spectacular things I've seen and done in my life. I saw so many impressive things—a man running with his kid on his shoulders; older runners like me; that sea of red shirts that never seemed to end. The other Carbon 14 runners and I had a wonderful time.

"My motto is and will always be: *Vida sana, cuerpo sano*—healthy life, healthy body."

PATRICK TOROITICH
TEGLA LOROUPE PEACE FOUNDATION
RAN IN NAIROBI, KENYA

Patrick Toroitich knows running can change lives. He works for the Tegla Loroupe Peace Foundation, named for Kenya's three-time world half-marathon champion. In her homeland, Loroupe is affectionately called "the athlete of social responsibility." Her Nairobi-based outfit holds races to bring together warring tribes in the country's northern Rift Valley and neighboring communities. Since the charity started five years ago, some 2,500 warriors, politicians and nomadic peoples have participated. Men and women compete in 10Ks; children run a 2K. Patrick helps oversee local programs dealing with poverty reduction, AIDS awareness and gender empowerment. Loroupe has a special interest in women's issues, especially among minorities and the marginalized. "The money we raise pays the school fees for girls in secondary school and supports local dispensaries and peace committees," says Patrick. Chauvinism against females has stifled the potential of Rift Valley girls. While sons inherit everything, parents view their daughters as a source of income, because they receive cows for their dowries. Education offers these girls a means of escape from a predestined life.

"My Human Race was amazing and funny," Toroitich says. "I had never experienced that much adrenaline and energy. At one point, a small child was keeping pace with me, and then he sped up and passed me as local elders stood around nodding and clapping as if I were an elite runner. This run encouraged me to run more … and to help society more."

SYLVIA WONG
CONCERNED CITIZEN
SHANGHAI, CHINA

"After the massive earthquake hit Wenchuan in May, I was desperate to go there. I volunteered for the rescue effort, but was turned down. When I found out that some proceeds of The Human Race would go to the earthquake relief effort, I thought this was the perfect opportunity for me to give my energy and spirit to such a worthy cause. The race took me almost two hours, but I enjoyed my run even though it was raining and cold. It was a great feeling; I don't think I'll ever get another opportunity like it."

LILLIE DOSS
RUNNER
AUSTIN, TEXAS

"I started running at age 64, when I weighed over 200 pounds. Now I'm 83 and weigh 118 pounds, and I feel great. Over the past 18 years, I have run about 750 races and accumulated 732 awards. I like to win, but running also keeps me in good health—body and soul. I am a 16-year breast-cancer survivor and ran a 5K just three weeks after that surgery. After I hit 70, I finished four marathons and three 50K ultra-trails in under the 10-hour time limit. What I really like about running is that I get to meet old and new friends; and everyone at The Human Race was so friendly and nice."

AUSTIN, TEXAS

FANG YUN-CHENG
FORMER SMOKER
TAIPEI

Fang Yun-Cheng had a troubled past, but running has given him a promising future. "I used to smoke too much and eat out too much and I never exercised," he says. "I knew I couldn't keep going on like that, so I started running and quit smoking at the same time. Whenever I had the urge to smoke, I'd go running. It worked great. I like running because you are always in control. I can run whenever I want to—I can run in the morning, in late afternoon, or whenever I have the urge to smoke. I run at least 10K every day." He now proudly points out that he is living up to his name: In Chinese, *yun* means "exercise" and *cheng* means "success." "I really love running!" he says. "Call me any time you need a running partner!"

ANA LUIZA DOS ANJOS GARCEZ
"ANIMAL"
SÃO PAULO, BRAZIL

"I learned to run to get away from the police," says Ana Luiza dos Anjos Garcez. "I was a street kid and I used to steal from people, then buy drugs." Her transformation into a champion runner began the day she saw an ad for a local marathon and decided to enter, even though she'd never run a race, much less a marathon. As she ran and ran that day, Dos Anjos Garcez desperately wanted to give up, but didn't because her friends, the other street kids, were cheering her on. (Her entry fee was paid with money the kids had stolen, and she snatched the shoes and shorts she wore that day from a clothesline.) She was one of the last runners to finish that day, but she did finish.

Some time later, she became entranced by a movie about running which was being shown on TV. The movie's theme song played in her head all day, she says, and that night, she decided to change her life. She sought help at a local free clinic, which sent her to a hospital. Tests there showed that she had the heart and lungs of a champion athlete. Dos Anjos Garcez started training seriously, and received donations after the local TV station ran a story about her. Her fierce determination and competitiveness got her off the streets for good. And earned her the nickname "Animal."

Now, Dos Anjos Garcez works on sports projects for children. She also finds time to run competitively: She holds the Brazilian record in the master's category for the 800 meters, 1,500 meters and 5,000 meters. "If it wasn't for athletics," she says, "I would be dead or—even worse—I would be in prison!"

TIM WIENS
"CLUB FAT ASS"
VANCOUVER, CANADA

"I was sedentary until I was 40. My younger brother wanted to run a marathon, and I thought, 'If he can do it, I can.' That's when I decided to make the lifestyle change, and I've been a runner for the last eight years—18 marathons and 21 ultra-marathons. Club Fat Ass, a local running club, has an event almost every other week; their big one is the Fat Ass 50 on New Year's Day, so many runners are hungover. We run a 50K and then jump in the ocean. Through the club, I meet oddballs who are into trail runs, double-Ironmans, or things like running rim-to-rim at the Grand Canyon. We have a 100-mile run along the sea coming up—the gold standard these days is 100 miles. The Human Race was shorter than that, but I enjoyed it. When I run ultras with Club Fat Ass, we always have lots of stories—encountering bears, wolves. A 10K is over so quick that there's not a lot to say, but I'd love to see the helicopter view of all that red pouring over the course. I felt like I was in an artery of blood flowing through the city."

KATINA "KITTY" TERRY
NIKE+ RUNNER
RAN IN COLUMBUS, OHIO

"In 1999, my junior year of college, a car barreled through an intersection and struck me. My car was totaled, and I hurt my back pretty badly—anytime I tried to run, a shooting pain would go up my legs, exhorting me to stop. So I did, for three or four years.

"Finally, desperate to run again, I started going to a chiropractor in Cleveland, driving two hours each way from Columbus twice a week. He said I had a slipped disc in my lower back. After regular visits with him, I was able to slowly find my footing again. I started running three miles sporadically, and it was a good two years before I could run five miles consistently.

"When the Nike+ equipment came out, I started using it right away. Inspired by my new equipment, I suddenly thought, I can do this. I ran eight miles that day and it felt great. Even more exhilarating was uploading that first run to the Web site to see where I ranked against others in the Nike+ community. The competitiveness of the other runners was infectious and I had to keep up. I had to run even farther. Eight miles felt so good that soon I was doing 10. And then 10 felt so good, I thought, 'Might as well do 12.' Now, I'm averaging about 15 to 20 miles a day on a 7:56 pace; I should hit 10,000 miles on the 31st, if not sooner.

"People ask me all the time, 'Why do you do it?' There's no doubt running has made me a healthier person. All that time I wasted, afraid of hurting my back instead of wishing it to get better, I finally went out and pushed myself and made it better. I never thought when I started doing this that I'd be No. 2 in the world for total mileage on the Nike+ site, though. You might call that a happy accident.

"The best part about running The Human Race was knowing that thousands of people were running the same race somewhere else in the world for an amazing cause. The virtual aspect of my run—I ran by myself in Columbus—in no way diminished the experience; in fact, it made me want to run faster. It was really cool to go on-line afterward and see how I finished compared to the world. I have 109 miles to go to hit 10,000, and I will hit it next week."

MAURICIO JORGE TRIBIÑO
URBAN RUNNER
CARACAS, ECUADOR

"Running in Caracas presents many of the same inconveniences as other large cities—bad traffic, limited spaces for running—but in this city crime is a big factor. Last year I was running at 10 a.m. in the part of town known as Country Club when a couple of guys on motorcycles ambushed me and took my cellphone, my wallet and my iPod. What's worse is that they left but then realized they had forgotten to nick my watch, so they came back and took that too. When I finally tracked down some police they basically told me, 'You know this is a public street and anyone can drive down it.' It's crazy here. Now, when I run with an iPod I switch out the white headphones for black ones, so it looks like I'm listening to an ordinary MP3 player. The white wires are a dead giveaway. Clearly iPods are more popular with thieves."

24 HOUR FITNESS
NATIONWIDE

Twenty-five cities sponsored official Nike+ Human Races, and thousands of other places around the world were sites of Run Where You Are races, but the folks who ran The Nike+ Human Race at a 24 Hour Fitness gym figured out how to participate in the race by going nowhere fast.

With more than 425 clubs in 16 states, 24 Hour Fitness is the largest health club chain in the U.S. 24 Hour Fitness was a big booster of The Nike+ Human Race: It encouraged members to sign up for it, to train for it and to run in it. Some members trained for the 10K with runs that began and ended at their clubs; others did their training on treadmills. In fact, because the chain is the first to offer special Nike + iPod–enabled treadmills, some of those training runs were linked directly to the Nike+ Web site. In the weeks leading up to the various Nike+ Human Races, more than 700 real-life humans recorded 28,000 miles on the Nike+ cardio machines. Or "virtually" that many.

On race day, treadmills at 16 select 24 Hour Fitness clubs were connected to Nike+ so that members could run with the rest of the world while staying in one place. Nationwide, 24 Hour Fitness estimates as many as 180,000 of their members put their miles in for The Nike+ Human Race using treadmills in their clubs to help make history.

MÜNCH'NER G'SICHTER (FACES OF MUNICH)

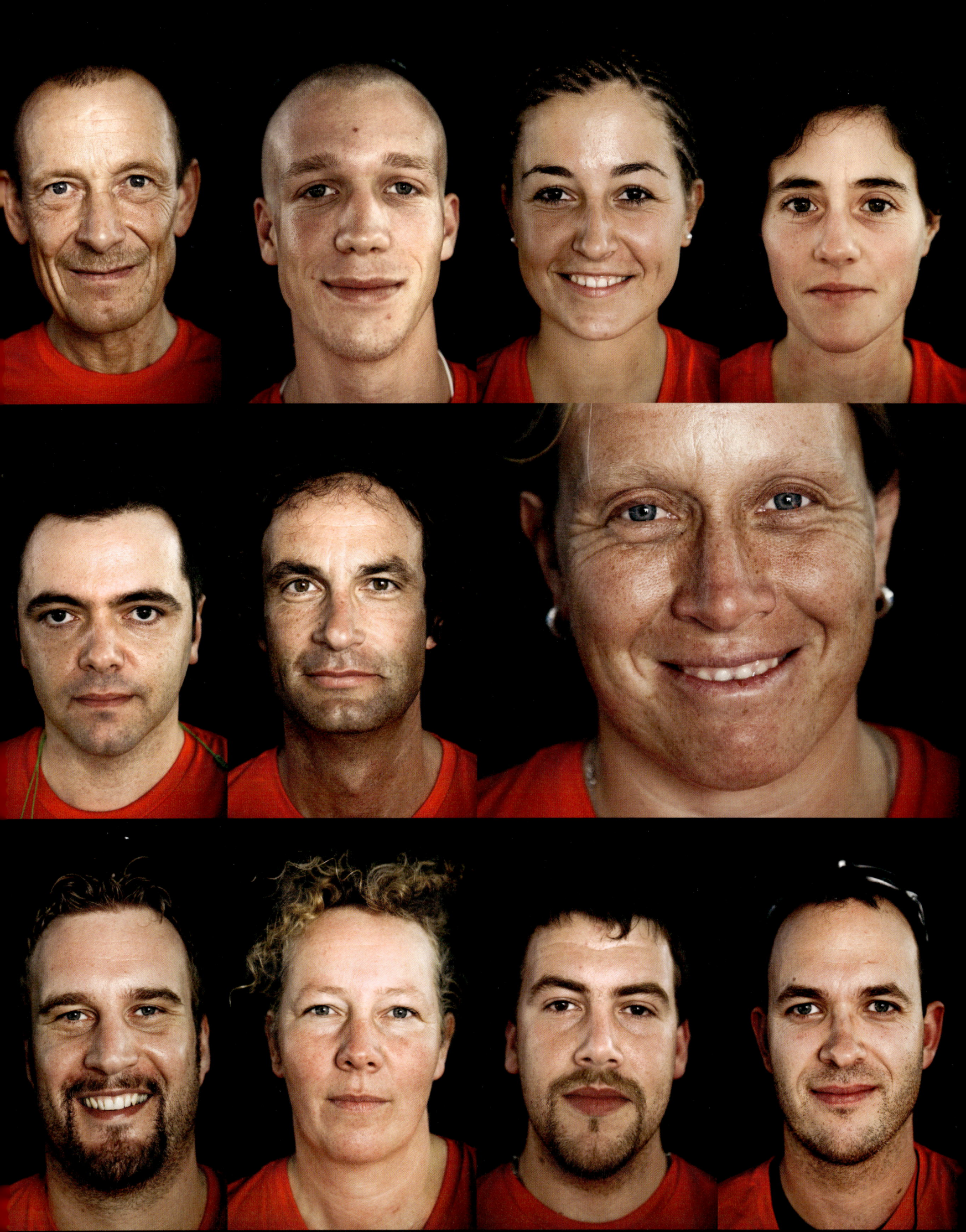

LANCE ARMSTRONG
LANCE ARMSTRONG FOUNDATION
AUSTIN, TEXAS

"The Human Race was a blast. I always like going for a run, but this one stands out in my experience because it was a good time for a good cause at the right time. It was also cool to see my hometown up-close, running down streets that are usually filled with cars.

"When I started out as an athlete, I ran in triathlons. During my retirement from cycling, I got into running in a new way. I competed in a few marathons, but The Human Race wasn't like any of those races—there was a sense of community I never felt at any marathon. As we started down Congress Avenue, I saw runners at all skill levels—hard-core athletes, weekend warriors and first-time runners—all running like they were possessed, fighting against the heat. It wasn't about who finished first, though, it was about finishing together. Regardless of their skill, the folks competing—and even the folks watching—seemed to know that this race represented something big.

"As I hoofed it through Austin, it made me happy to think that there were thousands of other cancer survivors around the globe running that day. I had been thinking a lot recently about how to take LiveStrong to the next level, to make the fight against cancer a global cause, and I had decided to return to competitive cycling with the intention of doing just that. As I was running, it hit me that the hundreds of thousands of people around the world running The Human Race were basically saying what I want to say: 'We can do this! We can change priorities! There is force in numbers!'

"I have always believed that the biggest obstacle to ending cancer is complacency. Cancer is an old disease. It's been around, and we're just used to it. Nearly 8 million people around the world will die of cancer this year. That number is not acceptable. With the resources we have, nobody should suffer from the disease in isolation or as the result of social stigma. When hundreds of thousands of people stand up and put themselves on the line—even if it's just for an hour—that tells me this is a fight we can win.

"After the race, as I stood onstage cooling down, I was blown away by the crowd of thousands of runners milling around. My friends Ben Harper and the Innocent Criminals were about to put on a rock show for all of them, and I had to admire what we'd all pulled off that day. The people of Nike made it happen. They didn't see obstacles, they saw opportunities. They thought, 'Why not hundreds of thousands of runners? Why not a sea of red runners comparing their times to others around the globe?' They thought, 'Why not try to change the world?'"

SUSAN BOYER
MEMBER, "PERU RUNNERS"
LIMA, PERU

"I moved here from the U.S. six years ago to work at a school in Lima. My first day there, a colleague placed an article about Peru Runners on my desk. The group has been around for almost 30 years—they run at dawn, a hundred-plus people. Next to the story was a photo of a man named Gonzalo, who had founded the group. A few days after that, I went out running on my own and saw a huge group of people running in my direction, and one of them was Gonzalo. As he passed me, he said, in English, 'Do you want to run with us?' So I joined the group.

"Gonzalo and I got married a year later. Last week was the fifth anniversary of the day we met, so we stopped at that same spot and kissed. Now we have a son. His name is Gonzalo too, and I've pushed him in his stroller on our training runs since he was about 6 months old. He yells, '*Quiero correr con mis dos patas!*' which means, 'I wanna run with my own two legs!' The Human Race was his third Nike 10K. Running is in his genes.

"I started out way in the back, with Gonzalo in the stroller, so I was dodging the crowd, yelling '*Permiso, permiso!*' ('Excuse me!') a lot. Soon, Gonzalo started to scream '*Permiso, permiso!*' too. It was funny. When we were close to the end, Gonzalo said he wanted to run, so 100 meters before the finish line, I took him out of his stroller, but he just stood there. Then a dog flew past him and he ran after it. The crowd went wild."

MIKE CERVERA AND ROMAIN VENTANAS
VIRTUAL TRAINERS
PARIS, FRANCE

"I lived in Paris until about a year ago when I left to study in England," says Cervera. "I didn't run—I hated doing it in school—but last summer my sister's boyfriend, Romain, introduced me to the Nike+ system, so we started running against each other—him in France and me in England. With each challenge we staked some silly prize, like a DVD, to make us run harder. When I signed up for The Human Race, I asked Romain to run with me. It took some negotiation, because his work now makes it hard for him to train as much as I do, but he finally committed to it.

"Oxford, with its flats and hills, is a great city to run in, but it pales in comparison to Paris. I moved back recently, and there's nothing better than doing a 10-kilometer run and taking different routes every time. Now that I'm back in Paris I find myself running to rediscover my city. There's nothing like an appreciation for the urban landscape to push your limits. It's more eco-friendly than a car—and better than a bike!"

DANIELA RAIMAN
UNHCR, THE UN REFUGEE AGENCY'S
NINEMILLION.ORG CAMPAIGN
RAN IN DAKAR, SENEGAL

"I'm from Slovakia. I'm 32 years old, and I've been working with refugees for the past nine years. I've lived in Africa since 2002, working for the UN High Commissioner for Refugees. When I first moved to the Republic of Chad I stopped doing any physical activity. I was living in a town that had a heavy military presence, and my work was extremely demanding, with a daily two-hour drive out to the refugee camp over bumpy roads in 130-degree heat. Also, as a woman, I attracted too much attention on the two occasions I tried to run.

"When I moved to a much smaller village, the security was better, so I started running every day. The inhabitants of the village looked at me with suspicion; in their culture, running is not what women are supposed to do. But after a while, they would greet me when I ran. It was a good way to make myself known to the community, which, in turn, protected me. Two years ago, I moved to a bigger town, Abéché, where it was difficult to find a place to run—kids would throw stones and the security situation made it dangerous to run in the streets. Fortunately, there is a French military base in town, so I would go there very early—by 7:00 A.M. it was too hot to run—or in the evening, and circle the track.

"I moved to Dakar this year, where I knew it would be easier to run, even if it wasn't 100 percent safe. There is much more traffic in Dakar than in Chad, and I have to be alert for passing cars, motorbikes or horses—which gives running the right edge. I picked a special route for 08.31.08: I wanted the run to start in front of the UNHCR office, symbolically, as some of the funds raised would be for refugee children. As I was running along the beach, I saw a stray dog that looked friendly, so I waved at him jokingly to join me. The dog took it as an invitation to play and started to lightly nibble on my calves. I had to slow down to a walk, since the dog took any increase in my tempo as a signal for him to jump higher and nip some more. I found it quite funny but couldn't run until a man sitting nearby decided to help me out—he whistled the dog away.

"I felt very privileged during my Human Race run. Dakar is on 0:00 GMT, and when I had gone to the Nike site the evening before, I saw that quite a few races were going to start soon. When I logged in again 24 hours later to upload my run, a number of races were just finishing and some still hadn't started—and it struck me how truly global the event was.

"Running this race was the same as giving money to a charity, only you earned that money while doing something you love."

JOSIE DYE
RADIO HOST
RAN IN TORONTO, CANADA

"My family can't believe I ran The Human Race. We are not an athletic family; music is our life. I host a show known as "The Nooner" on 102 the Edge in Toronto. I play music 4 1/2 hours a day. But now, I've become an obsessive runner. I chose running because I can't do yoga—I can't relax enough for that. I run three or four times a week, but you couldn't call it training exactly—I usually have a cheeseburger right after I run. Once a week I take a long run, sometimes 10 kilometers, but I'm never in a hurry. I trained pretty seriously for The Human Race, though. At the Edge, we have been talking back and forth with Vancouver radio stations and turning this into a big competition. We've been making fun of each other and bragging about who will have the most runners in the event. (We will, of course.) I plan to run the race with my cell phone in hand so I can call the station with live updates. My listeners will get to hear what I'm thinking while I'm running in the largest race in the world. And they'll hear me panting, too!"

PRZEMYSLAW SALETA
HEAVYWEIGHT FIGHTER AND KICKBOXING CHAMPION
WARSAW, POLAND

"Last December, I had surgery to donate a kidney to my teenage daughter. For unknown reasons there were complications—I was in a coma for a week and barely survived. After I got out of the hospital, running helped me get back in shape. It was always part of my training as a boxer—I was Europe's heavyweight boxing champ and a world-champion kick-boxer. Now, every kilometer I run is a gift. It's an expression of joy that I'm still here and that my daughter, 14, can lead a normal life. She's about to take her first trip in two years—she couldn't travel before the transplant because she needed dialysis.

"A big reason I ran in The Human Race was to raise money for charity. I work with two foundations, one that encourages people to give blood and become organ donors, and another that makes the wishes of terminally ill children come true. The main reason there are too few transplants in Poland is because people are afraid they'll only have half a life. Another reason I ran is that I wanted to show everyone that after donating a kidney—and even being in a coma—you can be fit, and live life as you did before."

THOMAS D
RAPPER
MUNICH, GERMANY

"The Human Race was a rush. So many people running together for fun, fitness and charity. No competition. Personal goals were the reasons for running. The whole atmosphere pushed me and all the other runners to top ourselves and still run together and be one with the event. To play afterward, with my band, the Fantastischen Vier, was hell for my legs, but heaven for the thousands of people at the post-race party. I loved it."

DIRK NOWITZKI
DALLAS MAVERICKS FORWARD
MUNICH, GERMANY

"The timing for The Human Race was tough for me, coming so soon after I played for Germany in Beijing—I felt really tired, and unfortunately I was a little bit sick that day. I also have to think about my job—playing in the NBA: Running a 10K on paved ground would kill me, because I am too tall and too heavy, and the pounding on my joints would be far too damaging. But I wanted to be a part of this great event, so I ran the first and the last meters. I'm glad I did. It was amazing to see all those passionate people running and competing against themselves. I felt a powerful energy."

KIMBER OLIVER
BUSINESS MANAGER
CHICAGO, ILLINOIS

"The race was amazing! The beginning was a bit of a hassle because there were so many people on the starting line, and it took a while to separate the fast runners from the slower ones, but the run was so much fun. I was extremely happy with my time—I ran a 44:22, which is a personal record. The last cheering section along the route was the highlight for me. It came at around mile 5.5, when I was really shutting down. They put a smile on my face all the way to the finish!"

JUNG WOO JIN
PHYSICAL EDUCATION TEACHER
SEOUL, KOREA

"The Human Race became a huge part of my social life and a major motivator for me to improve my health. I joined the 30-day training program Nike offered and I'm now running at least 5K every other day. My speed is improving, and I can feel myself getting stronger and healthier. What's even better is that I have made so many friends through the training program. I finished The Human Race in about 45 minutes and I placed 177th, but I am friendly with almost everyone who placed ahead of me, because we all trained together. This race reignited my desire to run."

ALEJANDRO RIVERA
DOCTOR
BOGOTÁ, COLOMBIA

"I was a junior national cycling champion, but by the time I got married I weighed 350 pounds, and within four years I gained almost 200 more. I tried many diets—none of them worked. My self-esteem was destroyed. My wife and I were on the verge of divorce. Two years ago, my wife and friends ran a Nike 10K. I watched them go out to train at night, but the only part of their training I joined in was the carb-loading they did a few days before the event. After that, I decided to have stomach surgery. The surgery is not a miracle—you have to do a lot of work. For last year's Nike 10K, I was still very fat, but my goal was to just finish. When it started, I thought, 'In 10 blocks, I'll be dead.' But no—I went at my own pace, running 500 yards or so, walking 500 yards, drinking some water, and then running again. I saw the signs saying "7 KILOMETERS LEFT, 6 KILOMETERS LEFT." After a while I was walking the whole time, but when I saw the sign that said there was only one kilometer left, I started to run. When I crossed the finish line, all my friends were waiting for me. It was a huge celebration—it was beautiful. The Human Race felt different, because I'm not afraid anymore. My wife finished five minutes before me, but I managed to finish before my mother and brother-in-law, which would have been impossible a year ago. I would like anybody in the world trying to overcome a physical problem to think about my story—you can achieve almost anything if you really want to."

WEST POINT CADETS
TRAINING RUN
WEST POINT, NEW YORK

"Upon entering basic training at the United States Military Academy in West Point, I was exposed to the joys of 'smoking oneself,' or running until exhaustion," says Charles Nadd (not pictured). "I was never a big-time runner and, coming from Florida, I was not accustomed to making my way up and down hills. Now I love running outdoors; it makes me feel like I am part of the world from which I come. I stay motivated to run because I know my profession will demand it of me, but when I am out there pounding the ground beneath my feet, I never forget to look around in awe."

BHUTANESE REFUGEES
UNHCR, THE UN REFUGEE AGENCY'S
NINEMILLION.ORG CAMPAIGN
RAN IN NEPAL

A nighttime monsoon that ravaged the southern Nepalese countryside—threatening high temperatures and even worse humidity at daybreak—gave way to thick clouds and an unseasonably cool dawn that had runners breathing sighs of relief as they converged on the starting line outside Damak. In small groups they came, on foot, veering off the Mahendra Highway (Nepal's major east–west thoroughfare) and spilling into the bordering rice fields as policemen brandishing old rifles tried to funnel them into a line where they could claim their yellow T-shirts and race-number bibs. The runners were quiet, but eager. Most of them were Bhutanese refugees who'd come to run their version of The Nike+ Human Race, hoping to draw attention to their plight, and to have a little fun. "Too many children like me in the refugee camp are just doing nothing," said Dil Maya Magar. "I want to be an example for them, show them that we can enjoy life."

Many didn't have proper running shoes, and some were barefoot, but they were all determined to run. "My father told me that he once ran in a marathon in Bhutan," said Parmila Ranapanelle. "I want to experience what he experienced, and show him that I can run and finish too. I wish I could run a marathon in Bhutan instead of running this race as a Bhutanese refugee in Nepal."

The run was organized by the Office of the UN High Commissioner for Refugees and CARITAS Nepal in collaboration with local organizations, and was partly funded by the FC Barcelona project for sports. The participants, ages 18 years and older, included Bhutanese refugees, Nepalese nationals and international NGO staffers working in eastern Nepal.

The women, most of them in their 20s, began 10 minutes before the men at an improvised starting line—a rope stretched across the highway's two lanes. They playfully bumped and elbowed for an advantage behind the rope, then after a shout of "Go!" shot forward to start their 7K run. The men, who would be running a 10K, weren't quite as orderly as they waited for their "Go!"—there was plenty of grabbing and tugging as they jostled for position, and a few shirts got ripped.

Ragged, distant mountains stabbed the sky to the north, and palm and banana trees that radiated green shrouded the blacktop. Volunteers on motorcycles raced ahead to keep the road clear of stray herds of goats, cows and water buffalo. Supporters lined the highway—some were elderly farmers in traditional dress, but most were half-naked children who jogged along with the runners for a few seconds before they gave up, wheezing with laughter. Soldiers in the Maoist People's Liberation Army broke ranks to jog alongside the runners too, but stopped when their commander ordered them back into formation.

As the day wore on, the morning cool gave way to a harsh and unforgiving afternoon heat, and the humidity started to take a toll. All runners were doused with a bucket of water as they crossed the finish line. The winner was awarded a cash prize of 20,000 NPR ($310 U.S.), though the biggest reward might have been just getting to run. "I participated in this race to show the world that we are stuck in refugee camps, but we are still strong," said Ago Raj Gurung. "I hope the race will put us in the spotlight again, so people will not forget us."

"I WAS NERVOUS TO RUN IN LAFAYETTE BECAUSE OF HURRICANE GUSTAV, BUT I WAS DETERMINED TO COMPLETE THE HUMAN RACE IN HONOR OF MY UNCLE HOWARD, WHO RECENTLY PASSED AWAY DUE TO LUNG CANCER. I RAN TO RAISE MONEY FOR LIVESTRONG."
—BRAD MICHAEL BECNEL
LAFAYETTE, LOUISIANA

"I WAS NOWHERE NEAR READY TO RUN A 10K, BUT I FELT I NEEDED TO BE PART OF THIS MOMENTOUS DAY. I FOUND MY RUNNING SHOES HIDDEN IN THE BACK OF THE CUPBOARD AND PUSHED MYSELF THROUGH DRIVING RAIN AND ANKLE-DEEP PUDDLES TO BE A PART OF HISTORY. IT WAS A PROUD MOMENT. I JUST HOPE MY SHOES EVENTUALLY DRY."
—DAVE DYSART
NORFOLK, ENGLAND

"IT WAS SO WONDERFUL TO RUN THE HUMAN RACE IN CHICAGO, AND TO BE CHEERED ON BY MY WIFE, DAUGHTER AND THREE SONS. A YEAR AGO I WEIGHED 283 POUNDS AND WAS READY TO BEGIN A REGIMEN OF BLOOD PRESSURE MEDICINE. HOWEVER, THROUGH STRICT DIET AND RUNNING, I AM NOW 175 POUNDS. COMPLETING THE 10K IN UNDER ONE HOUR WAS AN ACCOMPLISHMENT I HAD NEVER EVEN DREAMED ABOUT. BUT WHEN I LEFT THE STARTING LINE AND SAW MY WIFE, I FELT SO ALIVE! I PLAN ON RUNNING WEEKLY AND WILL ALWAYS REMEMBER THE THOUSANDS OF PEOPLE WHO I RAN WITH THAT SPECIAL EVENING OF AUGUST 31."
—WALTER FINDYSZ
WORTH, ILLINOIS

"I ALWAYS RUN WITH MY CAMERA, SO I CAN TAKE PICTURES ALONG THE ROUTE; AND I NEVER MIND STOPPING TO GET AN INTERESTING SHOT. I WAS RUNNING WITH THOUSANDS OF RUNNERS IN THE SINGAPORE LEG OF THE HUMAN RACE AND I SPOTTED THIS COUPLE TAKING THEIR WEDDING PICTURE. SO I STOPPED, TURNED BACK, PASSED MY CAMERA TO THE WEDDING PHOTOGRAPHER AND ASKED HIM TO TAKE A PICTURE FOR ME AS WELL."
—LIM PUEH TIAN
SELANGOR, MALAYSIA

"I TRULY ENJOYED RUNNING IN THE HUMAN RACE. IT WAS MY FIRST 10K! WAS IT EASY? NO! I RAN AROUND MY NEIGHBORHOOD, BUT I'M VERY PROUD! MY HUSBAND EVEN MADE ME A MEDAL!"
—NICOLE RICHARD
QUEBEC, CANADA

"BEFORE THE HUMAN RACE, I HAD ONLY DONE A 5K, SO I WAS REALLY CHALLENGING MYSELF WITH A 10K. BY THE TIME I COULD SEE THE FINISH LINE, I WAS WALKING, BECAUSE I HAD STARTED TO FEEL SICK. A MAN RAN UP BESIDE ME AND STARTED CHEERING ME ON, SAYING, "COME ON! LET'S GO! YOU CAN DO IT!" SO I BEGAN RUNNING AGAIN, WITH COMPLETELY RENEWED ENERGY. I RAN AT TOP SPEED, WEAVING MY WAY BETWEEN RUNNERS. I COULDN'T EVEN FEEL MY LEGS. IT WAS THE MOST EXHILARATING PART OF THE RACE: A COMPLETE STRANGER GAVE ME THE SUPPORT I NEEDED TO CROSS THAT FINISH LINE. THANK YOU SO MUCH, MY CHEERING STRANGER!"
—AMANDA POGATSCHNIK
CHICAGO, ILLINOIS

"I RAN IN THE HUMAN RACE BECAUSE I WANTED TO PROVE TO MYSELF THAT I COULD DO IT. THIS WAS MY FIRST RUN AND MY GOAL WAS TO FINISH THE RACE WITHOUT WALKING. AND I DID! I RAN THE WHOLE RACE AND FINISHED IN A LITTLE OVER AN HOUR. NOT BAD FOR MY FIRST 10K!"
—BRIDGET CAMERON
NEW BRAUNFELS, TEXAS

"I RAN THE MOUNT FUJI LEG OF THE HUMAN RACE. WHAT HELPED ME FINISH WERE ALL THE SUPPORTERS WHO HELD OUT THEIR HANDS FOR A HIGH FIVE AT FIVE KILOMETERS. WHEN I SLAPPED THAT PALM WITH MINE, MIRACULOUSLY, IT WAS AS IF I HAD BEEN CHARGED WITH A FRESH BURST OF ENERGY. WHEN I FINALLY SAW THE FINISHING POINT ON THE OTHER SIDE OF THE LAKE, ALL THE FATIGUE THAT HAD ACCUMULATED DISSIPATED. THIS WAS MY FIRST 10K BUT WILL DEFINITELY NOT BE MY LAST. WITH EACH STEP I RAN, THE FARTHER I LEFT MY OLD SELF BEHIND, WITH NO REGRET."
—TERENCE CAYDEN FONG
SINGAPORE

GILBERT TUHABONYE
"GILBERT'S GAZELLES" AUSTIN, TEXAS

For just a moment, Gilbert Tuhabonye looks sad. "I was very disappointed not to run in Beijing this year," he says softly. "I really wanted to retire." Before he can finish the thought, however, he's interrupted by a friend's daughter, who announces to Gilbert, "You make me laugh!" In an instant his 1,000-watt smile returns, and he's joking around with her, then singing a hymn, "Victory in Jesus," inspired by his shoes—a pair of Nike Zoom Victory+'s. "When I was training in Burundi," he says later, "we'd go on long runs and make up songs—about girls, anything. We all sang. We'd come home and I'd feel like a singer, not a runner."

Disappointment at not making the national team is understandable; that he would retire from running is shocking. After all, it saved his life. On October 21, 1993, Gilbert, 18, was herded into the shell of a building in Burundi with the rest of his Tutsi classmates. The Hutu mob outside waved machetes while others hurled burning branches into the building. Tuhabonye was beaten and burned; he expected to die that day. Desperate, he grabbed the charred femur of a dead friend, broke a window and ran into the night. As the genocide spread across Burundi and, later, into Rwanda, Tuhabonye convalesced in a hospital. It would be a year before he regained his strength and came to the United States to train. He was an All-American runner in college, and now has a reputation in Austin for good humor and good coaching. His training club, Gilbert's Gazelles, has nearly a thousand members, including hundreds who participated in The Nike+ Human Race. As did Gilbert. He hoped to finish in the top five, but coaching now gives him a bigger kick than individual achievements. "I would be a loser not to run this race," he says. "This is The Human Race; it's more than a race."

Gilbert finished second in Austin, behind a runner he's been competing against all his life—his brother.

ALEXANDRA BRAUN
PUBLICIST, TELEVISION HOST AND FORMER MISS VENEZUELA
CARACAS, VENEZUELA

"It was marvelous to feel the same energy and share the experience with thousands of people, all running in the same event. The Human Race was the first time I ran a 10K, and now I intend to register for other races to prepare for next year's Nike race."

JULIAN TOOHEY
ACCOUNTANT
MELBOURNE, AUSTRALIA

"After sitting in the office drinking coffee all day, it's good to get outdoors and run it all out of my system. It felt very different running through the streets of Melbourne in The Human Race—the lack of cars and hordes of runners presented a stark contrast to what I see when I go in there to work every day."

FRANKIE CHEN

"I was a *seifeizai*, or 'dead fat boy.' I have celebrity cousins, movie stars, and that's what they used to call me. I grew up with them, but they didn't impress me. Celebrities aren't happy—they're under endless pressure to be popular in a phony world. But as a 175-pound teen, I wasn't impressed with myself either. I had breasts back then.

"I've been a volunteer ever since. Four years ago, I came to Taiwan, and my friend Aaron and I started Team Live Right, a charity that promotes early education and cancer prevention. I love my life now. And running is still vital for me. My friends say I get grumpy if I don't do it. When I run, I don't worry about what people think—I'm centered on my dreams."

AND AARON BERG
CO-FOUNDERS, "TEAM LIVE RIGHT"
TAIPEI

"At 27, I discovered I had melanoma and only a 50 percent chance of surviving. As a father of four, the diagnosis and then the treatments had me slipping into depression. I needed a goal to inspire me, so why not a triathlon? I joined a running club—you really need friends to pull you out the door when you want to sleep in. (My take on The Human Race: It was amazing to see how many people dragged themselves out of bed at 4 or 5 in the morning to run it!) Sport is more than exercise: It creates a passion for overcoming challenges. Pessimism is the norm when life hurls difficulties at us; but in running, when you see the hill, you want to tackle it. You feel powerful and free.

"My full-time work now is teaching cancer prevention in seminars, with Frankie, through an organization we call Team Live Right."

AMI AYALON
CABINET MINISTER
RAN IN TEL AVIV, ISRAEL

Ami Ayalon is a minister in the Israeli cabinet and sits on various committees relating to national security. "When I started running in the hills near our small farm 20 years ago, people looked at me strangely. Now, people are running all over the place. Now, you see a culture of healthy living growing here, even though we're all consumed by the daily struggle to survive."

He was commander of an elite, physically-demanding military unit from the age of 31 to "the very advanced age of 35"—"advanced," that is, in a unit in which most members are in their early 20s. "I've kept very fit all of my life out of necessity; with me it became a way of life. In my family, there is a culture of exercising one hour a day, every day, whether it's running, cycling or swimming. From the day my sons were able to decide what they liked to do, they've been running, riding bikes and driving tractors, skiing, you name it." Every year, Ami and his sons (ages 27, 30 and 33) do a physically challenging event together. Last year, they swam the length of the Sea of Galilee. Sometimes they go on ski trips to Europe. This year, Ami and his three sons decided to run The Nike+ Human Race together.

For security reasons, Ami cannot mention his sons, who have all served in elite military units, by name. "When I look at my three boys, I say to myself: I don't need bodyguards. I'm very proud of them." (But he does have bodyguards, several of whom ran with him in the race.)

"Usually I prefer running on my own, so the experience of running with so many people in The Human Race added a thrilling element. Of course, getting to the finish line with my boys also added something very special to the experience. We weren't running to win, we were taking it easy; although if the boys hadn't been running with their dad, I think at least two of them would quickly have gotten antsy and wanted to pull ahead. They're pretty competitive guys."

# ERIC PERAKSLIS
LANCE ARMSTRONG FOUNDATION
NEW YORK, NEW YORK

"I'm a full-time cancer researcher; I've had a tremendous amount of cancer in my family, and I'm a stage-three kidney cancer survivor. When I got the diagnosis four years ago, running and biking became my therapy and also my revenge: To press myself and know that I was getting stronger was a way to take control of what was happening to my body. In the hospital for my surgery, we learned that I'm sensitive to pretty much every narcotic painkiller, so after the operation, when I was hurting, they couldn't give me anything—all I could do was get up and move. First I'd walk around the house, then on the treadmill, and then I got strong enough to jog for a few miles. It's a cliché, but with exercise, you always feel better when you stop. You say, 'Well, my side may be hurting from the surgery, but at least I'm not running anymore.'

"When I first got involved with the Lance Armstrong Foundation, it was raising money in the Tour of Hope. I accidentally fell into a community of people who knew what I was going through, who had either been there themselves or had helped somebody through it. I see The Human Race as a metaphor for the suffering that my family and I have gone through. To watch people overcoming their personal battles is amazingly uplifting. I'm a back-of-the-pack runner, and to see people pressing themselves is a testament not only to health but to spirituality."

FACES OF ROME

"I had a collision in Piazza di Spagna, but I kept running, and I felt very much a part of the race. Never stop! You always need to arrive at the finish line." —Roberto Zenca

EMILIANO OROZCO AND ALEJANDRA SARMIENTO
MOTHER AND SON RUNNERS
MEXICO CITY, MEXICO

Emiliano Orozco, 6 years old, ran a 3K leg of The Nike+ Human Race with his mother, Alejandra Sarmiento. "Emiliano really enjoys running, and he is a much better runner than all the kids in his school," his mother says. "I started when I was 10 years old and it has been a great part of my life; I recently ran a marathon in San Francisco. But Emiliano started even younger, when he was 3, so he has the chance to become a really good runner. If he wants to compete in the future, that would be great. But if he just wants to run for health and fun, that would be great too."

RICHARD CARROLL
WWF
RAN IN ST. MICHAELS, MARYLAND

"People call me the 'silverback gorilla' because of my rough gray beard, my thick gray locks and because I run with apes for a living. As the managing director of Congo Basin, Namibia and Madagascar, for WWF, I see that the task before us is as monumental as the cause is urgent: In the Congo, if current deforestation trends persist, 70 percent of the region's forests could be lost by 2040, and because the Congo Basin holds up to one-quarter of the world's tropical forests, this not only threatens the silverback gorilla's survival, but risks irreparable damage to one of the most important wilderness areas on Earth.

"I grew up on a small farm in rural Connecticut, with a naturalist for a mom. After finishing my undergraduate studies in marine biology, I joined the Peace Corps. I ended up in the Central African Republic; lived in small villages, learned the local languages and culture, taught fish-farming, then went into the wild to follow rhinos and elephants.

"During my years in the jungle, I had several near-death experiences from staph infection, malaria, dengue fever, charging elephants and a mislabeled bottle of embalming fluid that I mistook for water. I'm now pre-embalmed, so I may live forever. I still shudder at the memory of getting chased by lions while riding a small 175 Yamaha motorcycle on an elephant trail.

"With gorillas, you have to do everything you can not to run. I don't care who you are: If you try to make a mad dash, they'll pursue you like linebackers, take a bite out of your backside and scamper off with a rump roast. The only way to ward off a gorilla is to stand your ground, divert your eyes so as not to stare and then act like a monkey—which comes somewhat easy for me! Gorillas are smart, funny, beautiful creatures. Glimpsing a gorilla through the green veil of the jungle, catching its eye and sensing the species connection made me realize that if we humans cannot protect our nearest relatives, then we have failed as a species.

"In the early 1980s, I walked more than 1,000 miles in the jungle, studying gorillas and other wildlife. It was surprising to see that the main primates active in the forests were loggers, slicing and dicing their way through the gorilla habitat. I persuaded the Central African Republic to outlaw hunting, with an allowance for the indigenous people using traditional spears and nets. In 1990, the area was declared a national park and reserve. Even better, 90 percent of the revenues from tourists in the park go to local communities. They now realize that the wildlife is more valuable alive than dead.

"When I was younger and lighter, I loved to run, especially on woods trails. As an older silverback, I'm not as fleet of foot, but fitness allows me to be with the people of the forest personally and passionately, and to help ensure that their ways survive. The Human Race was a great opportunity to help raise awareness about the fundamental role WWF plays in preserving the critical biodiversity and helping the peoples of the Congo Basin forests."

GUILLERMO PALACIOS
"SUPER AZUL"
LIMA, PERU

"I've always wanted to be a superhero. At night as a boy, I prayed I would wake up with new powers. When I was studying fine arts in college, I was given a project to develop my alter ego, and I came up with 'Super Azul'—the Great Blue One. The mission of Super Azul is to rescue himself from himself, mostly by running. Through him, I recapture the qualities I had as a child: sincerity, transparency, the ability to have fun and be amazed. As Guillermo, I'm always getting into trouble—arriving late and having discipline problems—but Super Azul's job is to get me up and running, because runners always have excellent discipline. I play soccer and run three times a week, and when I play sports and run, I convert into Super Azul. I also do workshops for children where they create their own superheroes. It's a way for them to get to know themselves and identify the qualities they want to develop.

"I dedicated The Human Race to my 6-month-old nephew, who was born with a breathing defect and is now fighting for his life. During The Human Race I absorbed all the positive energy and channeled it. I wore a special cape with my nephew's name on it—and after the first half of the race, I released the cape, sending all the good energy I had picked up out to him. This race is just the beginning of a series of races dedicated to someone in need. That is Super Azul's new mission."

LONDON, ENGLAND

ASHLAND HIGH RUNNERS
CHICAGO, ILLINOIS

The town of Ashland, Ohio, has one fire station, one police station, six parks, 25 traffic signals and 24,000 people. For a town that size, though, it has a suprisingly large number of former residents who have made their names in sports, from auto-racing to professional football.

On August 31, four lesser-known Ashland athletes arrived in Chicago to join The Nike+ Human Race. Tim Black, the Ashland High boys cross-country coach, and Ashland Middle School track coach Brian Kettering made the six-hour car ride with AHS senior cross-country runners and team captains Jarrod Heydinger and Kelsey Snively. "To us, The Human Race is both a worthy charity and an adventure," says Kettering. "How often do you get to go to the big city and run?" At 31, the eighth-grade American Studies teacher had only been to Chicago once before, and that was in high school. "In those days, I was running cross-country," he recalls. "That may have been the year we won the Ohio Cardinal Conference and finished fourth in the state."

Black and Kettering had run marathons in Cleveland and Columbus, but never in a 10K this big. Heydinger and Snively had never run a 10K, period. Fortunately, Snively was going to be in Chicago anyway. "Kelsey's folks were planning to move his older brother into school over that weekend," reports Kettering. Adding a race into the mix made perfect sense to them.

Taking part in The Nike+ Human Race was Black's idea. "Tim said, 'Let's do something on the fly,'" says Kettering. Which apparently comes naturally to Ashlanders. Back when two big balloon manufacturers were based in town, Ashland billed itself as the Balloon Capital of the World, and it's now home to a hot-air balloon festival. "I don't know a lot about the balloon event," says Kettering, "I do know this summer was the 19th running of that."

Running, he knows.

LUCKY TWO-TIMERS
MELBOURNE, AUSTRALIA AND
LOS ANGELES, CALIFORNIA

Just once—at the start of the L.A. leg of The Nike+ Human Race—did Adam Perry think that taking advantage of the International Date Line to run two 10K races in the same day was stretching life beyond its natural resiliency. "The first two miles, I was saying 'Why am I bothering to do this?'" Then he pulled himself together and ran a 42:46, very close to the 42:30 he ran on a hilly, more challenging Melbourne course earlier that same—but very long—day. Perry, a 25-year-old tax lawyer from New York City, was one of five runners who won a raffle to fly to Melbourne, with a guest, to run The Nike+ Human Race there on Sunday, then get on a jet, land in Los Angeles around 3 P.M. and run that city's Nike+ Human Race five hours later. For many of the double-runners, the time change (Melbourne is 17 hours ahead of Los Angeles) produced a dreamlike state that lingered as the 8:31 P.M. race drew near. "Yesterday was a long day," Perry says. "We didn't know what time it was or where we were."

Forty jet-setting runners took part in the Melbourne–Los Angeles dual duel. Some slots were set aside by Nike to honor the efforts of corporate partners. Starbucks, for example, sent Tani Mintz, a barista from Skokie, Illinois, who says training for The Nike+ Human Race reawakened a dream to be a top speed skater. The "airborne to run" vibe was so powerful that even the three Air New Zealand pilots ran the Los Angeles leg of The Nike+ Human Race.

After the second race, shouting to be heard over the pulsating music of Kanye West, the two-timing 10Kers celebrated their time-warped accomplishment. Reggie, who runs about five miles a day with a Nike training club in Los Angeles—"Running is like medicine to me," he says—was the star of the delegation as members congratulated each other. "This was one of the highlights of my running career," he says. "I don't feel jet-lagged." Reggie's energy might have been due to the adrenaline, or to his outstanding conditioning … or to the comfortable seat he had on the flight to Los Angeles—he won an upgrade to first class for identifying Nike's original name, Blue Ribbon Sports.

IGNACIO GARIBAY
BULLFIGHTER
MEXICO CITY, MEXICO

Ignacio Garibay and his wife ran The Nike+ Human Race with their 18-month-old son in a special three-wheeled buggy they use on all their runs with him. "He likes it most of the time," says Garibay. "But if he starts crying, we have to stop to give him a bottle. I wasn't too worried about him getting hurt during The Human Race, because everyone was polite and well-mannered. This is a great, fun event. Fighting bulls, on the other hand, is scary and remains scary no matter how long you do it."

CHUCK JONARD
LEADER, NIKE+ MILES WALKED¹ IN LODI, CALIFORNIA

"In 1977, I was in a really bad car accident. Our convertible rolled and the impact tore off part of my arm and riddled my upper back with shards of glass and rock. My doctors eventually recommended amputation of my leg and hospitalized me in the VA ward with the quadriplegics and paraplegics. Over time a theme emerged with these guys: 'If I could just walk again.' It was as if none of them realized they had this gift until they lost it. After knocking on that door, I made a vow to myself to make the most of my gift when I recovered. And I have.

"I always enjoyed walking, but since I got the Nike+ equipment, I've sort of taken it to the extreme. This year I made a pledge to do 500 miles a month, averaging 20 miles a day (which I break down into smaller components). In fact I walk so much that the Nike+ system has a hard time keeping up with me—last year, I had to replace a Nano and three shoe sensors. I know a lot of people on the Nike+ Web site are thinking, 'How can this guy do all these miles?' Well, I'm just some old guy with bum legs and joints, and I'm sure there are people in Third World countries who are leaving me in the dust ... except they don't have a Nike+ to measure their efforts. The big thing that I get a kick out of is when people ask me, 'Are you running all day long?' If I were running all day long, I'd be even slower. Maybe like two hours a mile. If I'm lucky.

"I walked my 10K for The Human Race early in the morning, alone. I knew I could not be the fastest in the race—or even fast—but I was hoping to make a good show on miles. It looks like I will put in 60K today—maybe a little more, but then again, maybe less. Today was a good day."

SARAH REINERTSEN
TRIATHLETE
LOS ANGELES, CALIFORNIA

In 1992, 17-year-old Sarah Reinertsen was watching the Ironman Triathlon on TV when an extraordinary idea popped into her head: She decided she was going to be the first female amputee to complete that notoriously brutal race. She knew that several male amputees had finished the event, and she said to herself, 'I know a girl can do that, and I want to be the one.' Sarah just had to get over a few minor hurdles, such as not knowing how to ride a bike or swim. And she had never run a marathon.

In October 2005, the lonely girl who was shunned on the playground because of her disability finally realized her goal in the Hawaii Triathlon. "It was a dream I carried for a long time," says Reinertsen, who eventually moved from her native New York City to Mission Viejo, California, so she could better train for the physically demanding race. "It was almost a 13-year goal for me to get to that finish line."

Reinertsen was born with proximal femoral focal deficiency, a condition that caused her left leg to be so badly deformed that it had to be removed above the knee when she was 7. Four years later, a female amputee and runner changed her life when she introduced her to an amazing athletic world where girls just like her were competing in races. "She became my role model," says Reinertsen. "She had done nine marathons, so always in the back of my head was the idea, 'I want to do a 10K just like Patty.'"

Reinertsen now tries to share her experiences—and triumphs—with other amputees. "I do a lot of clinics where I teach amputees how to run, because I know how important it is. When someone leaves the hospital after an amputation, there is the question, Now what? I'm trying to fill that gap for them. I wasn't always included in sports and games as a child. By running in The Human Race I have a chance to remind people that we all need to help get people with disabilities off the sidelines and into the game.

"The L.A. Human Race was at night, and I'd never done a night race before—I really had to pay a lot of attention to where my feet were—but I had fun. There were cancan dancers and Japanese drummers along the course, which made it a celebration of the whole world. The race had this beautiful feeling of unity. I believe running is a celebration of being alive, and that's what I was thinking about as I ran."

ANNE MAHLUM
FOUNDER, "BACK ON MY FEET"
RAN IN PHILADELPHIA, PENNSYLVANIA

"I grew up in North Dakota and moved to Philadelphia several years ago. On my morning runs I noticed a group of men standing on the corner of 13th and Vine, so I did what you do in North Dakota: I waved at them. They waved back. The next morning I did it again. I started looking forward to seeing them—soon, they knew my name and they'd wish me luck on my run. Every day I'm running past them, waving and smiling, and then I realized that I'm leaving them in the exact same spot every morning while I go home and move my life forward spiritually, mentally, emotionally and, of course, physically. I know what a powerful motivation running can be, and I wanted to share that with these men. I looked up the name of their shelter and called the director and said I wanted to start a running club: Back On My Feet. This was in June 2007.

"I sent out an e-mail to anyone I could think of, asking for shoes and running clothes. Soon, people were sending in donations as well. It was really cool. The first day, there were just nine homeless guys. I talked about what running has meant to me and laid down some guidelines for being a part of the running club. Then we stretched and ran a mile and stretched again. From that, it has grown to four teams in Philadelphia, each one organized through a shelter. They run at between 5:30 and 6 in the morning three times a week.

"Mike Solomon has been involved since Day One. His wife had just died when I met him, and he had a past of drugs and alcohol and incarceration, and he wanted to get away from all that. He started running and doing more miles. He ran in the Philadelphia half-marathon. He also started studying at the Metropolitan Career Center, which is one of Back On My Feet's education partners. Mike had never touched a computer before, but he graduated from that program in May. (He ran the Delaware Marathon in May as well.) He got hired for a part-time job by a survey research firm. The shelter he was living in saw what everybody else saw in him—that he was dedicated—and they hired him too. Mike now works two jobs, full-time at the shelter and part-time for Back On My Feet. Last weekend, he moved into his own apartment. This is the first time he has lived on his own and he worked really hard for it.

"When someone with a job calls and wants to know about a team member, it gives me no greater pleasure than to tell them this person is out there three days a week at 5:30 in the morning. It shows your respect for yourself, it shows you know how to be part of a team, that you know about perseverance. Those are qualities employers look for.

"I'm happy to report that 33 Back On My Feet members ran in The Human Race; it was a great opportunity for us to give back—and to support three great charities—by making our miles count for something more than just distance."

JOYCE SERPAS
THE FINAL FINISHER
LOS ANGELES, CALIFORNIA

Joyce Serpas didn't want to do The Nike+ Human Race. "I'm not a runner. I don't walk. I don't do anything," says the 31-year-old native Angeleno. But her best friend, a die-hard runner, wouldn't relent. "Do this race, it's for cancer," she told Serpas.

In July, Serpas started working out at the gym, walking on the treadmill. But the morning of the race, she woke up with butterflies. "I almost didn't go," she says.

When the starter's horn sounded in Los Angeles at 8:31 P.M., Serpas and her friend took off with 13,000 cheering runners into the gritty streets surrounding the Los Angeles Memorial Coliseum. Then her friend sprinted ahead. "I started running the first mile," Serpas says. "Then I just walked." But she soon found herself captivated by the spirit of the event. "I didn't realize until I got there that all these cities were participating. It was amazing how many people I met. Everybody was really friendly. People on the street were cheering for me. There were little kids dancing."

Still, as the course stretched on, she wasn't sure she'd be able to finish. "I almost gave up twice, but I saw a lot of people trying hard. There were people like me who are heavy, and they were doing it. That inspired me. I kept telling myself, 'Just finish!'"

By 10:15 P.M., Serpas was almost the only runner on the course. "There was someone a few feet in front of me, and by that time, I wasn't bothering to look back. I remember thinking, 'I wonder if I'm alone?' I got a little bit scared, but then I turned my head and saw that a Nike truck was beside me."

She completed the 10K in 2:03:18. When she finally walked beneath the towering red Nike+ Human Race banner at the finish line, Kanye West was singing "Homecoming." By then there was no announcer or crowd to celebrate her arrival, but she didn't care. "I was really happy. I felt good about myself because I didn't quit. As long as it took me, it still felt good to finish."

After meeting up with her friend by the beer stand, the two of them sat on the cool grass and listened to Kanye West perform his final two songs. "I loved the concert," Serpas says. "That was one of the main selling points she used to convince me to do the race. It motivated me to continue working out. I think we're already going to sign up for a new walk."

THE MAKING OF A RACE

Hundreds of thousands of people ran in The Nike+ Human Race, including several thousand in Austin, Texas. But The World's Largest Running Event didn't just happen. It took an army of professionals and volunteers more than a year to do it right.

Labor Day Weekend, 2007: Jean Gordon, brand manager of running for Nike's southern division, arrives in Austin to scout out the city. She's based in Miami, but knows Austin has a lot going for it: a city-managed web of running trails; an active running community cultivated through support groups such as Gilbert's Gazelles and Rogue Training; high profile boosters of running such as Lance Armstrong, Mayor Will Wynn and Texas Governor Rick Perry; the energy of more than 90,000 university students; its reputation as The Live Music Capital of the World. "But I needed to feel it for myself," says Gordon. "Could we really pull off a 10K race knowing it will be very hot that day? Would local events like BatFest! and the University of Texas home opener football game overwhelm our race?" And the answers were 'yes' and 'no'—Austin's a special city when it comes to running and music."

Other big factors in Austin's favor are the strong, longstanding relationships Nike has with the University of Texas and with the Lance Armstrong Foundation, one of the main charities supported by the race.

Gordon consults leaders in the local running community about the logistics of staging a world-class race. In Austin, that means Paul Carrozza, John Conley and David Grice. Carrozza, owner of the popular Run-Tex store, chairs the mayor's task force for road races in Austin; Conley and Grice run local race-production companies and have handled events such as the Austin Marathon. "I've worked with John and David for decades," Carrozza says. "We couldn't have asked for a better situation. That doesn't mean it was easy."

December 2007: Course director Grice submits to the city the first of dozens of permits and bundles of paperwork needed to hold a race. "This is the first time we've used this course," he explains. "Nike needed a common start-finish line because of the post-race concert, and they wanted it to be in one of the city's iconic locations. We need a course that is exactly 6.2 miles, with streets wide enough to handle all those runners. The city, rightly so, requires police and EMS on-site. Plus, about 10,000 people live downtown, and they need to be able to get to their doors. This may be a global event but it has to be managed at a block-by-block level."

May 2008: Ashley McLean, Nike's local "Ekin" (a community relations position that requires her to know the brand backward and forward) begins to educate local retailers about the race. "Every Foot Locker, every Finish Line, as well as the dedicated running stores like RunTex and Rogue Equipment—I was there," she says. "If someone bought a pair of shoes between now and August 31, 2008, I wanted the store to tell them about the race."

July 2008: The Nike team begins its push to get thousands of runners registered. "I went to my retailers, twice a week, gave them buttons and information cards. I made sure they knew all the details," Ashley says. A first call for volunteers is posted on craigslist.

August 17, 2008: The U.S. men's swim team wins the 4 x 100 medley relay, which puts Brendan Hansen and Aaron Peirsol, University of Texas-Austin alums who committed to The Nike+ Human Race in April, on the winner's podium and on the front page of newspapers across the country. With Lance Armstrong, concert headliners Ben Harper and the Innocent Criminals and two high-profile gold medalists, the Austin race now—officially—has star power.

August 21: Hundreds of runners file into the Tap Room at Six Lounge in Austin's lively Warehouse District. In minutes they will file out again for a training run led by Nike volunteers, one of three this week. Some have already registered for the race; others are here for the free barbecue and beer, and the chance to try some Nike shoes and other gear. More than 300 runners register at this event.

August 24: A local BBQ restaurant begins smoking the 250 pounds of beef and 120 pounds of sausage they expect to sell on race day. "The smoking's the easy part," says Jennifer Robin. "Chopping all that meat so it can be made into sandwiches—that's work."

August 29: Construction crews begin building the stage in front of the State Capitol, where Ben Harper and the Innocent Criminals will headline the post-race party/concert. Meanhile, Ashley and her team of recruiters are handing out to returning UT students burnt orange T-shirts with the race logo WHERE WILL WOU BE? along with socks. (What student can't use an extra pair?)

August 30: The first of 160 portable toilets is placed along the route. Chain link fence, plastic cones and water stations are also unpacked. Grice has his team paint orange rings around potholes on the course so runners won't be tripped up. He also persuades city workers to fill a few potholes on Second Street.

At the UT football game, the scoreboard video screen shows a rowdy group waving signs, AUSTIN VERSUS THE WORLD! 8-31-08.

August 31, 8:00 A.M.: Congress Avenue is closed to traffic. JumboTrons and loudspeakers squeal as they're plugged in. In a hotel's ballroom, video teams are downloading footage of The Nike+ Human Races already run in Taipei and Melbourne for racers to watch after they finish.

10:00 A.M.: Governor Perry's office calls to say he can't make the race because he needs to prepare for the thousands of people who might be evacuated to Austin if Hurricane Gustav hits Texas.

4:28 P.M.: "Lance Armstrong is here!" says Erica Pedreguera, Nike's public relations manager, as her team swarms to greet him in the hotel's lobby.

6:28 P.M.: World champion swimmer—and official race starter—Aaron Peirsol exits his hotel room with his Nike escort. He walks to the start line, raises an air horn high and starts the party.

6:41 P.M.: Someone in the Nike command center on the second floor of the hotel speaks quietly but urgently into his headset: "Do we have any available golf carts? Matthew McConaughey's girlfriend needs a ride to the next cheering zone, a-sap!"

6:43 P.M.: Thirteen minutes into the race, Emily, a local triathlete, sprints down Seventh Street and hands off videotape shot near Mile Two to another courier, who charges through the crowd toward the ballroom. There, Daddy Van Production crew will cut footage from the first third of the race, producing a "thank-you" video tribute to the Austin runners that will be shown at the end of the show by Ben Harper and the Innocent Criminals.

7:40 P.M.: The last runners have crossed the finish line, and sports drinks and bananas give way to beer and barbecue.

9:58 P.M.: Ben Harper and the Innocent Criminals show goes off without so much as a busted guitar string, and he puts poetic punctuation on things with his final song, rallying the crowd one last time: "I can change the world, with my own two hands ... gonna make it a safer place, gonna help the human race ... with my own two hands!"

10:10 P.M.: Volunteers walk (and regularly stop and stoop) along Congress Avenue, putting the last of 35,000 plastic water bottles into recycling bins. The street is clean within minutes. "Austinites actually look for recycling bins when they finish their bottles," says Grice. "Environmental awareness is high here. That helped a lot with cleanup."

10:20 P.M.: Congress Avenue begins to empty, the heart of Austin literally pumping red-shirted runners into the night. "That's it," says Jean Gordon. "We did it."

—E. CASEY KITTRELL

(Above left): Con Mi MADRE works to keep Austin's Hispanic girls in school and focused on getting a college education; it also tries to strengthen their family relationships by involving their mothers in the pursuit of those goals.

(Above center): Tents of Hope is a community-based response to the crisis in Darfur, in which volunteers paint canvas refugee tents with images of hope, love and peace. After the tents have been used to raise funds and to increase awareness about the genocide in Darfur, they will be sent to Chad and Sudan, where they will become homes and classrooms.

(Above right): The Fugees Family, based in Atlanta, helps the young survivors of war rebuild their lives by running soccer and education programs for refugee children from 24 countries.

YOU'LL NEVER RUN ALONE AGAIN

Running can change how you look. It can change how you feel. It can even change how you think. It doesn't affect people the way earthquakes and wars do, but it is important. It can even change the world.

When you run alone, you learn about yourself. When you run in a group, you learn about working together, about sharing and caring. When you run with the world, you learn about the importance of community, about transcending creed and color to come together for the benefit of all.

Which is precisely what happened all over the globe on 08.31.08. Hundreds of thousands of people ran 3,189,429 miles in 25 cities and raised millions of dollars for the WWF, The Lance Armstrong Foundation and the UN Refugee Agency's ninemillion.org campaign. The headline of a London daily cheerily described the event as GLOBAL SWARMING.

And all of those runners, we did something just as important as raising money, something that can't be measured but can't be ignored.

There's a well-known short story in which a character hopes to save the planet from the brutality of World War II by staging a rugby match. That's pretty much how the former army major, Alejandro Rivera, saw his run in Bogotá, Colombia (p. 157). Rivera jogged the entire course on one foot; he lost the other to a land mine in San Vicente del Caguán, a jungle region in southeast Colombia controlled by antigovernment guerrillas. "My wife got to the finish line five minutes before me," he recalls. "But I managed to get there before my mother and brother-in-law, which would have been impossible for me a year ago. I would like anybody in the world trying to overcome a physical problem to think about my story. I know it's possible to achieve almost anything if you really want to."

Everyone in The Nike+ Human Race seemed to have an inspiring story, if only because everyone who ran was part of this story. Mauricio Jorge Tribino, who ran in Caracas, Venezuela, felt that: "With my friends and mother cheering me on, I crossed the finish line in 53 minutes and now I have my medal," he says. "It's fascinating to know that hundreds of thousands of people felt the way I did today. I thank Nike for uniting hundreds of thousands of crazy runners like me from all over the world."

Thousands of those crazies came together in Munich, Germany, where Gunther Weidlinger of Austria claimed The Nike+ Human Race crown by posting the world-best time of 29:25, and Angela Roerkohl, a German triathlete who placed fifth in Beijing, outpaced all women in 31:09. Curiously, the top three Nike+ runners were on treadmills in gyms all over the world—with faster marks than the road racers. No word on whether they set their machines on "decline."

In Rome, track and field legend Carl Lewis, whose 10 medals include nine golds, challenged more than 7,000 entrants to "run like they have never run before." In addition to the participants, the Roman route was packed with thousands of concertgoers—which equaled the number of runners who filled Wembley Stadium in London to hear a pre-race set by Moby and Pendulum. Sent on their merry way by the great British marathoner Paula Radcliffe and middle-distance champ Sebastian Coe, the throng threaded through the streets of London despite a bucketing rain, and still finished with the fifth-best aggregate time of 57 minutes and 58 seconds.

Thousands of runners showed up in Warsaw, making The Nike+ Human Race the largest 10K ever in Poland. The event was sold out long before the start. "People who normally don't run very much decided to take part even though they had trained too little to cover 10 kilometers easily," says Szczepan Figat. "But the atmosphere of the event—people supporting each other, shouts and applause from onlookers lining the route—put wind in their sails."

Much the same spirit infused Istanbul, Turkey, a city where, it's been said, "running doesn't happen." Thousands of runners made it happen, though, by taking to the streets and crossing from Asia to Europe over the Bosporus. Itir Erhart (p. 100) says: "That moment of running over the Bosporus Bridge—against an indigo sky, with the monuments lit on the shore, the sound of the boats, the smell of the sea, the refreshing breeze and the thousands of runners pausing to admire this magical scene—will be forever engraved in my memory."

That spirit ricocheted all over the planet like a viral call to arms—and legs—even galvanizing people who ran by themselves. It touched Chuck Jonard (p. 192), who walked his 10K not long after the sun came up in Lodi, California, to beat the heat, and Daniela Raiman, a Slovakian woman working for the UN High Commissioner for Refugees, who ran in Dakar,

Senegal (p. 144), where it is impossible to beat the heat. And impossible for her not to feel that she was involved in something bigger than her, bigger even than all of us. Chuck and Daniela—and 10-year-old Emiliano Orozco in Mexico City, Mexico (p. 180) and 95-year-old Horacio Caggiano in Buenos Aires, Argentina (p. 114)—all know that after The Nike+ Human Race, they'll never run alone again.

As many philosophers have noted, humanity is a work in progress. In other words, as Kenny Moore wrote in "Why We Run" (p. 290), we aren't even restrained by our genes, nor our Darwinian imperatives. We can do better, be better. And as The Nike+ Human Race proved, we can make the world run better.

That news came as a joyous revelation to Phil Cha, who ran in Seoul, Korea (p. 181). "I was running hard and fast," he says. "Then an old woman passed by me, effortlessly. I had to laugh. And I saw that everybody had a smile, too, laughing and happy for their own reasons. I felt a national pride when the race began, thrilled to see Koreans active and fit. By the end, though, I found myself thinking about how runners around the world are feeling this same pride and joy today. We gathered in our respective cities, surrounded mostly by our own respective races, but as we raced together, we transcended that and ran as a human race."

BEHIND THE SCENES AT THE RACES

A SMALL SAMPLING OF WHAT IT TOOK TO PULL OFF THE NIKE+ HUMAN RACE.

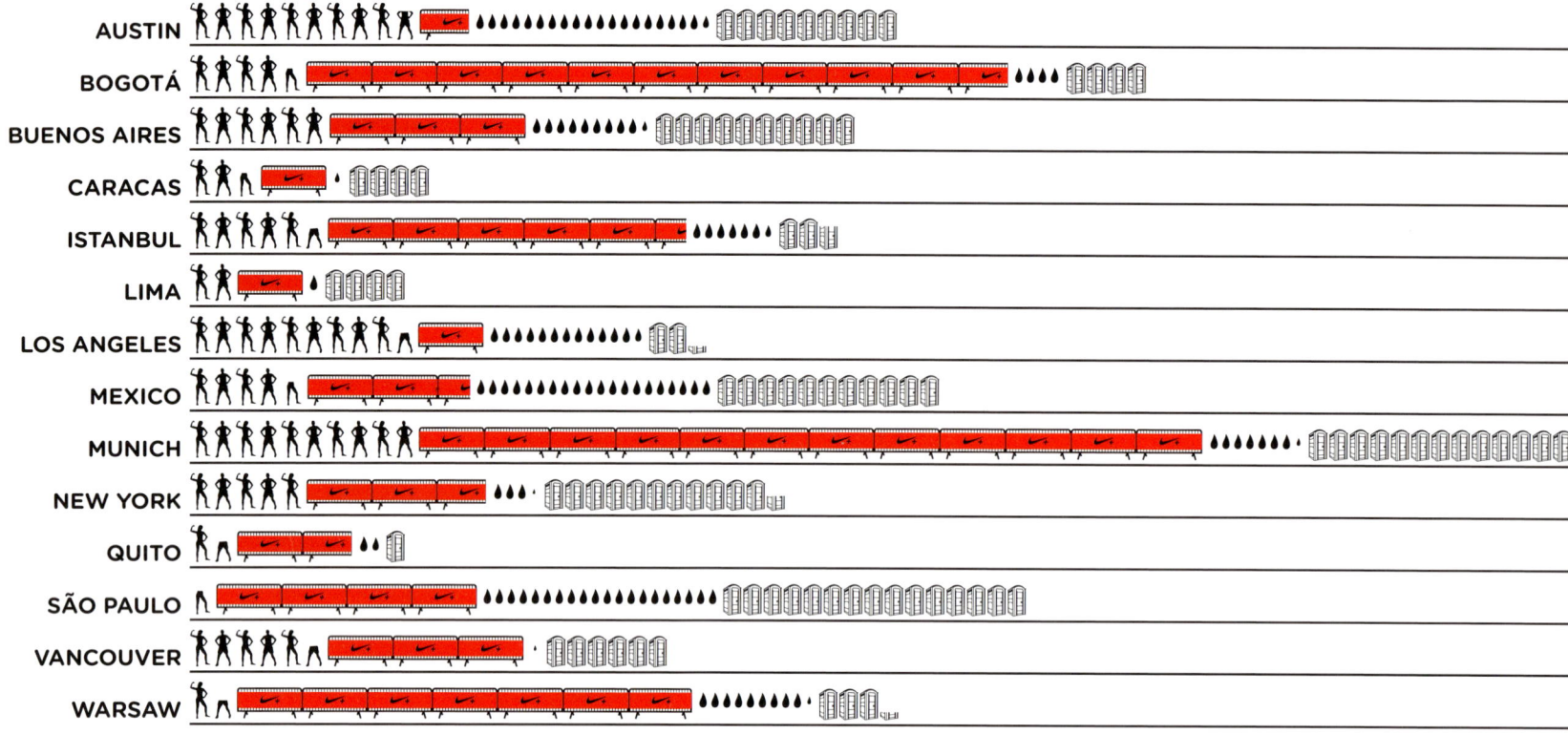

GLOBAL INDIVIDUAL BESTS

TOP 10 FASTEST WOMEN

01	Nadia Rodriguez	Buenos Aires	744812	33'58"
02	Valeria Rodriguez	Buenos Aires	745290	34'13"
03	Vincenza Sicari	Rome	80501	34'14"
04	Chengcheng Jiang	Shanghai	9374	34'16"
05	Karina Cordoba	Buenos Aires	742628	34'22"
06	Giovanna Volpato	Rome	89688	34'30"
07	Zenaide Vieira	São Paulo	503274	34'32"
08	Azucena Díaz Calvo	Madrid	58107	34'34"
09	Olga Kimaiyo	Mexico City	86020	34'35"
10	Xueqin Wang	Shanghai	21343	34'41"

PHOTO FINISH

IF EACH CITY WAS A SINGLE RUNNER, HERE'S WHAT THE FINISH WOULD HAVE LOOKED LIKE (BASED ON THE CITIES' AVERAGE PACES).

City	Average Pace
Madrid	56'34"
London	57'48"
B. Aires	58'03"
Vancouver	58'22"
Rome	58'31"
Portland	58'33"
Munich	58'51"
Paris	58'52"
Melbourne	58'58"
Quito	59'37"
Warsaw	1:00'43"
Lima	1:01'22"
Mt. Fuji	1:01'40"
Chicago	1:01'59"
New York	1:02'08"
Sao Paulo	1:02'45"
Los Angeles	1:05'22"
Mexico City	1:06'05"
Bogotá	1:06'35"
Seoul	1:11'35"
Austin	1:11'51"
Taipei	1:12'05"
Caracas	1:12'26"
Singapore	1:14'24"
Shanghai	1:16'54"
Istanbul	1:18'57"

TOP 10 FASTEST MEN

01	Gunther Weidlinger	Munich	1715	29'25"
02	José Manuel Martinez R	Madrid	910254	29'39"
03	Julius Keter	Mexico City	188624	29'50"
04	Gilberto Silvestre Lopes	São Paulo	510904	29'52"
05	Hillary Kimaiyo	Mexico City	93871	29'53"
06	Simon Bairu	Vancouver	531	29'55"
07	Reyes Estévez López	Madrid	949599	29'59"
08	Mariusz Giznski	Warsaw	64159	30'00"
08	Danny Kassap	Vancouver	576	30'00"
10	Luiz Fernando de Almeida Paula	São Paulo	516422	30'01"

217

LIMA, PERU

AFTER THE FINISH LINE...

FIREWORKS ON THE BOSPORUS
ISTANBUL, TURKEY

Some in Turkey doubted The Nike+ Human Race would be a success there. "My friend joked that there was no way Turks would pay to run in anything," one happy runner exclaimed after he crossed the finish line in Istanbul. Thousands of others—friends, family and the curious—lined the streets to cheer runners on. "Go, women!" some of them cried, showing solidarity with runners who risked scorn in a society that isn't always happy to see young women galloping down the street in short-shorts.

Massive fireworks heralded the runners as they finished. The tired but jubilant horde then stretched and cooled down on Istanbul's twinkling coastal road before slowly making its way down the red carpet into the Turkcell Kuruçeme Arena, on the European side of the Bosporus. From there, runners and revelers could gaze across the river and see Asia, where they had begun their journey that day. Above their heads, lit up like a Christmas tree, soared the famed Bosporus Bridge, which they had all joyously run across, symbolically linking East and West with their feet.

Even before the after-party began, the crowd was percolating with energy, bouncing to house music blasting through the speakers, showing off dance moves to their friends. Exhausted but giddy runners rejuvenated themselves with water, candy bars and beer, just in time to dance again to a live performance by Kenan Dogulu, one of Turkey's hottest pop stars. When he took the stage, young girls and old men began mouthing the lyrics of his songs and dancing.

"Here's to The Human Race," a 38-year-old runner said, lifting his beer in a toast. "I've been a proud member of it since 1970."

TRULY GRANDE FINALE
LOS ANGELES, CALIFORNIA

When hip-hop king Kanye West took the stage beneath the bright eternal flame and iconic rings of the Los Angeles Memorial Coliseum, it was hard not to reflect on 1984 when athletes and entertainers from around the world came to Los Angeles, and united its sprawling, multicultural neighborhoods. There were affluent University of Southern California co-eds and Hispanic children from L.A.'s poorest neighborhoods. There were fathers pushing baby strollers and grandmothers with teenage granddaughters. Huddled together under the warm night sky, most sat on the vast lawn outside the Coliseum, the fluorescent bands they'd worn in the race still glowing in the dark. They might have been tired and sweaty, and their bodies sore from pounding the hard city streets, but they didn't act like it. They hooted, screamed and whistled as a very energetic Kanye exhorted the crowd to sing along, clap along or engage in some boisterous call and response. They—and Kanye—were jubilant from start to finish. After Kanye's hour-long set, the stage lights went down and the sky became filled with a pulsating shower of fireworks. Then suddenly, it got quiet and dark, and a sea of red T-shirts filed away slowly out of the park as the flame burned on.

FIESTA GRANDE
MEXICO CITY, MEXICO

After Mexico City's Nike+ Human Race, La Maldita Vencidad played a high-energy set next to the towering Angel of Independence monument. Thousands of runners standing in the street leaped up and down to the bouncy ska rhythms and shouted the lyrics to many of the group's songs. When the band played "Pachuco," many in the audience hurled plastic bottles of water into the air, creating a sudden (and fleeting) rainstorm that cooled off the crowd on a warm morning.

Lead singer Roco tore round the stage with an infectious energy and invited a dozen young runners to dance on stage with him, which they did in a dervish of delight. Horn player Sax was also going wild—on one song he shoved two saxophones into his mouth and played them both at the same time. Following that impressive trick, he threw himself into the crowd and was passed about on a sea of hands before being pushed back onto the stage.

At one point, the band asked the jubilant runners to raise their hands in a call for peace, a needed call in a country that has been shocked by a wave of violence this year. Nearly 3,000 people have been slain in drug-related killings since January and there have been hundreds of high-profile kidnappings. Hundreds of thousands of people had marched for peace from the same Angel of Independence monument the day before.

But even that somber reminder of strife couldn't dampen spirits on this triumphant day. When the show finally came to an end, the cheers were deafening.

MELBOURNE, AUSTRALIA

WRAP (RAP) PARTY
SINGAPORE

Singapore was the only Southeast Asian city to host The Nike+ Human Race, and interest there was so great that it was the first of the cities around the globe to close registration. Thousands of people ran, beginning with a dash over the bridge spanning the Singapore river; runners then turned west, hugging the south bank of the river before doubling back along the north side.

A lively after-party awaited runners who crossed the finish line. Runners rehydrated, stretched and gratefully sat for complimentary massages as the concert began. First up was a local mandarin rap group; they were followed by another rap act, which shrewdly worked in a few mentions of things identified with Singapore—"chicken rice," for example, drew a big cheer. Throughout the show, the hosts threw giveaways to the crowd, which gave everyone plenty of motivation to keep their eyes and attention on the stage. A sea of red shirts danced, sang along with local favorites and cheered lustily as Nike Singapore country director Stanley Goh gave out awards to the top men, women and youth runners. The run raised money for WWF, the Lance Armstrong Foundation and the UN refugee agency's ninemillion.org campaign.

Though the crowd of thousands was tired and in desperate need of showers, many stayed for the headliner, the Boston-based band Boys Like Girls. Their hit "Thunder" was an appropriate coda to a long and exuberant night.

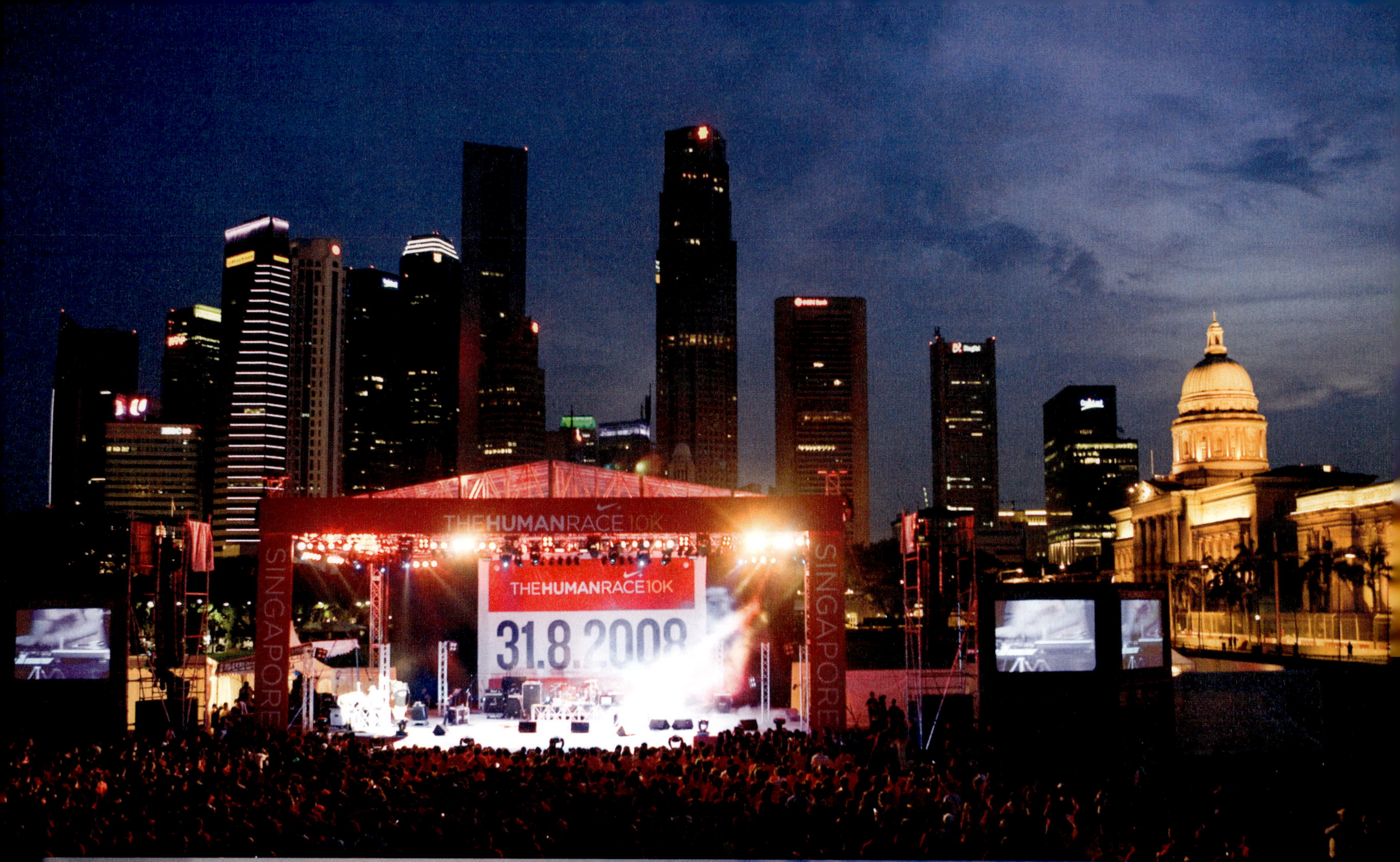
THEHUMANRACE10K
SINGAPORE
THEHUMANRACE10K
31.8.2008
SINGAPORE

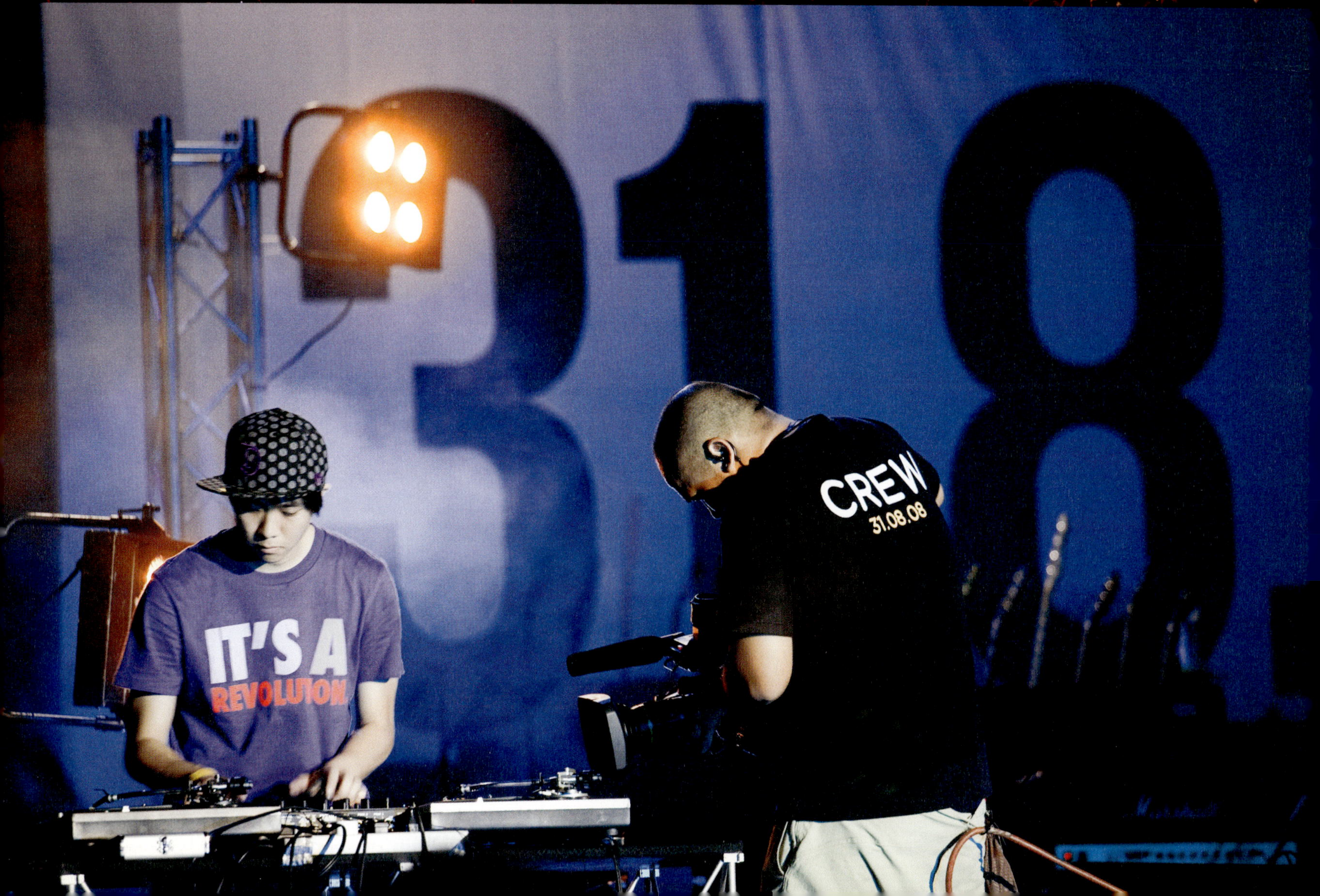
IT'S A
REVOLUTION
CREW
31.08.08

WHY WE RUN

We run because it's impossible to resist. As children, we can no more not run than a lamb cannot leap. As adults, when we are spurred into sudden motion by a looming taxi, we find ourselves the unsuspecting descendants of men who could run down a deer in a day. In every cell, every mitochondrion, every spurt of neuropeptide, we are coded to run, and to keep running.

Humans evolved into runners over the past two million years. We had no choice. Each time the species dwindled and faced extinction, the African continent spared only those who could stride for hours in the noonday heat, when hyenas could not, when lions could not. We also developed acute binocular vision. Predator's eyes. Within the deepest, vestigial nature of any runner is a wiry hunter trotting on the savannah, senses as sharp as an osprey's, ever alert for any movement, which could mean dinner or danger.

Given the primacy of that design, you'd think the question of why we run is easily addressed. But the answer is gloriously complicated.

Some of us run to race, to consume ourselves in effort, or to triumph, to wave from the podium. We race with profound gratitude because our means of deciding who wins are the clock and the camera, not some battle-axe gymnastics judge.

RUNNING THROUGH HISTORY

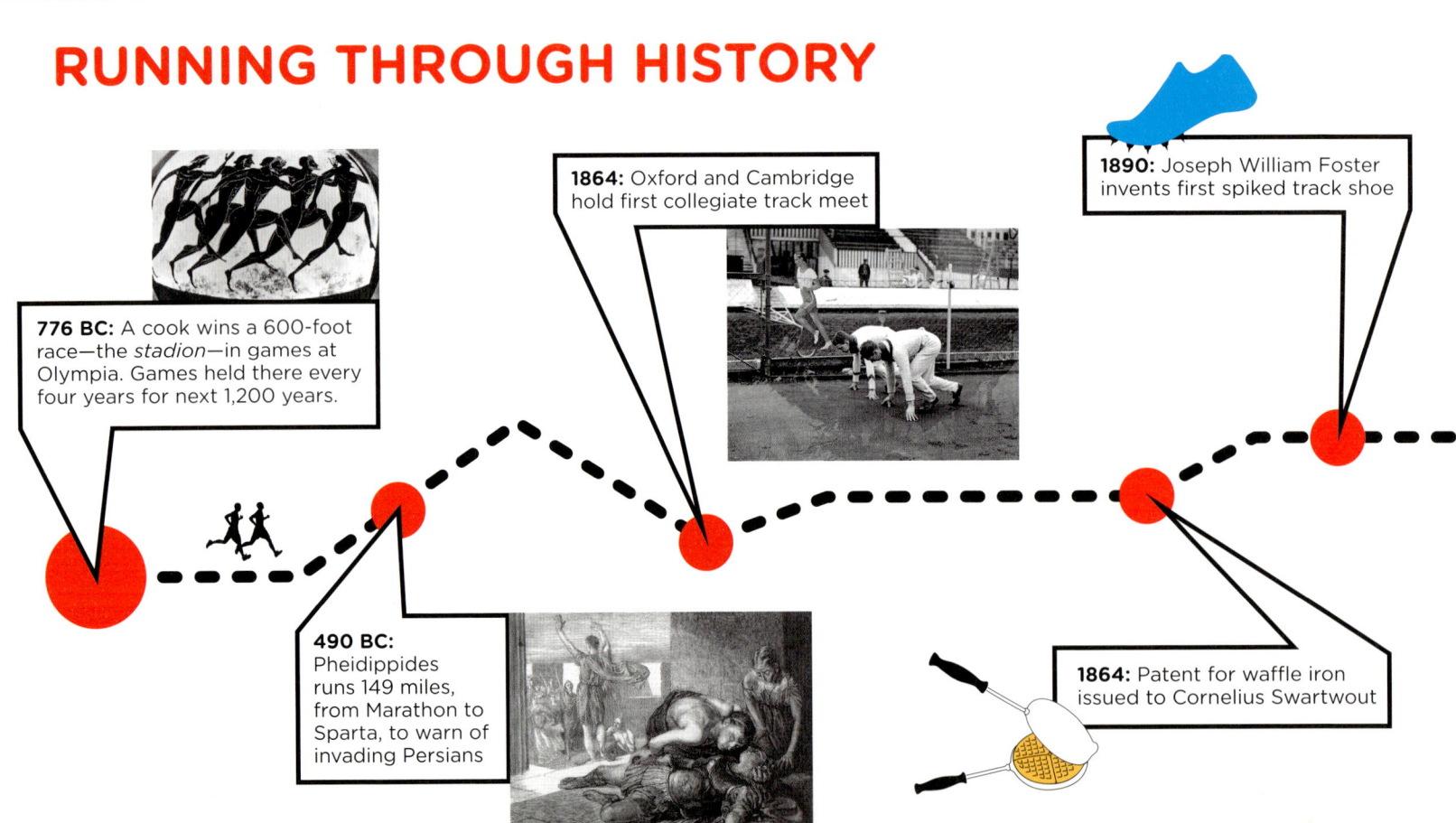

776 BC: A cook wins a 600-foot race—the *stadion*—in games at Olympia. Games held there every four years for next 1,200 years.

490 BC: Pheidippides runs 149 miles, from Marathon to Sparta, to warn of invading Persians

1864: Oxford and Cambridge hold first collegiate track meet

1864: Patent for waffle iron issued to Cornelius Swartwout

1890: Joseph William Foster invents first spiked track shoe

In any race, we are moved to our greatest performance in our greatest contests, but forcing yourself to death's door for a gold medal is not the same as chasing a gazelle so you don't starve. Racing lets us systematically explore our own limits and surpass them. It lets us compare generations. It leads to greater feats than the ancestors may have ever known.

We are no longer unremittingly Darwinian. We run to transcend, and even outgrow, our raw, reflexive competitiveness. Our prototypes had to be aggressively fearful. We don't. We can use running for anger management. All runners are mellower for having run, men and women alike.

The simple truth was revolutionary. Ever since swift Atalanta, women have yearned to run, but lived under patriarchs who thrust them onto pedestals or made them chattel. At no time before the last century have fathers encouraged their daughters to run or to be athletes.

It took pioneers such as the first woman to run a marathon in Boston, to prove that the world was suppressing a great legacy.

Set free, women proved they can cover every distance 90 percent as fast as the swiftest men; one woman now wins open 100-mile ultra-marathons

1908: Marathon distance set at 26 miles, 385 yards for London Games, in a race where Italy's Dorando Pietri staggered across the finish line first but was disqualified because he received assistance. The winner became 22-year-old New Yorker Johnny Hayes.

1937: German scientist Otto Bayer develops polyurethane

1896: Modern Marathon introduced to games as 40K run from Marathon to Athens

outright. Western society now offers women true parity for the first time since the savannah, and maybe ever.

While training to race we sublimate, we channel. At our best, we transform fears and regrets into medals and records. At our worst, we over-train, and slowly destroy our health. I once screamed at my dear friend Alberto Salazar because he was running a ruinous 100 miles during the week after winning the New York City Marathon. He now agrees, because he never returned to his best after that.

We run to recall the great champions we have burned into memory and compare ourselves to them. We run, therefore, to better appreciate the art of the winner of the Beijing marathon, who was more liquidly efficient in his 26th mile than he was in his first. Since we were all made by running, we are perfectly capable of imagining how his 2:06:32 felt to him—the feathery ease of his 4:48 miles—even if we've never done a single one.

We also run, as do the Zen monk marathoners of Japan, to make the gift of our endurance holy. There is no more exalted state, they say, than the moment of exhaustion before consciousness departs. I experienced something like that after a run of 43 miles. I felt myself a renunciate, sanctified, purged,

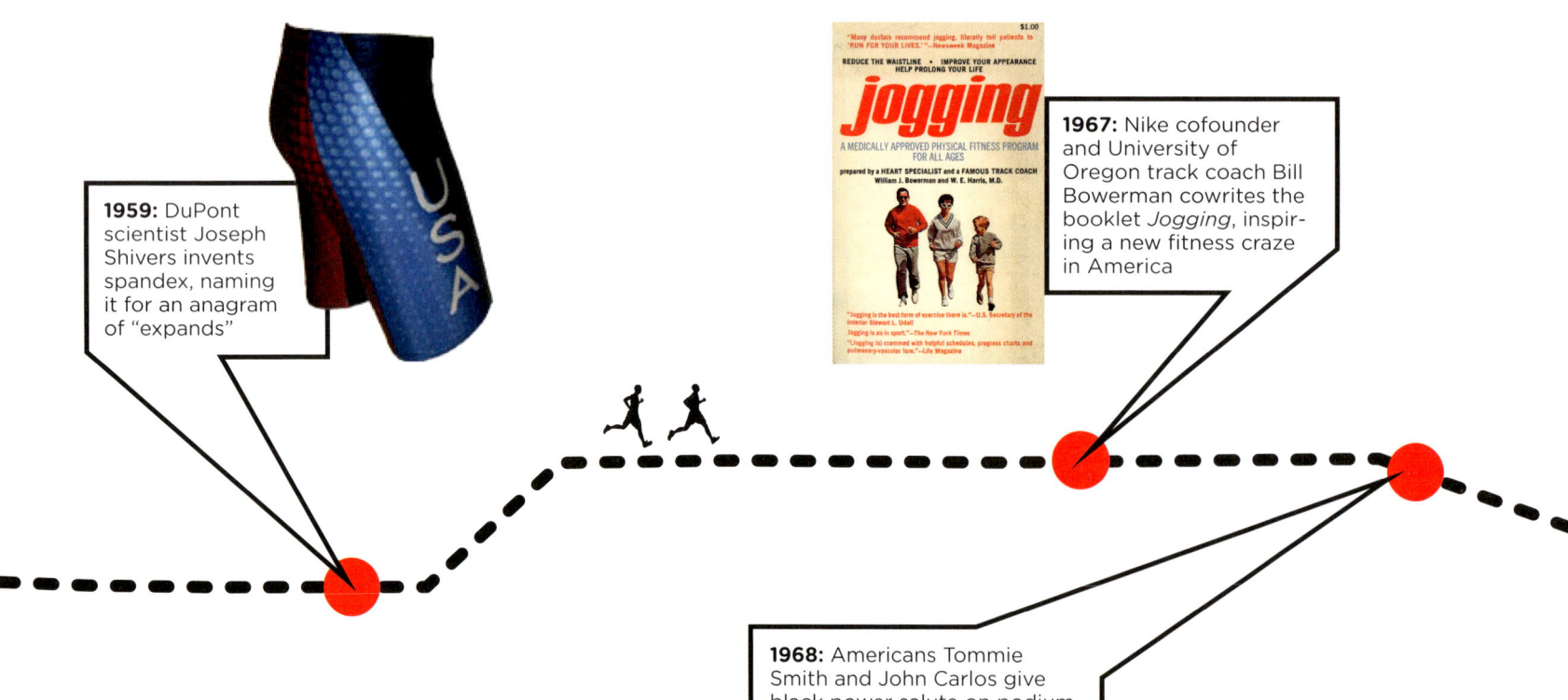

1959: DuPont scientist Joseph Shivers invents spandex, naming it for an anagram of "expands"

1967: Nike cofounder and University of Oregon track coach Bill Bowerman cowrites the booklet *Jogging*, inspiring a new fitness craze in America

1968: Americans Tommie Smith and John Carlos give black power salute on podium during 200m medal ceremony

shriven. Yet I was one with my fellow exhaustees. That of course is the spiritual ideal-apart from all; united with all.

This surely adds to the appeal of ultra-running on trails, such as the 100-mile Western States race. These runners show we can still be the ancients, still live up to their distances. Of course it's not like they ever left us. Distance runs are crucial to the Tarahumara Indians of Mexico's culture. The ability to run 200 miles on a handful of quinoa and a few gulps of creek water is still how they select the men to pass on their genes.

Because running is in every part of us, it shows up in every part of life—from solemn rite to frolic. Runners run to have fun with the dogs, to speed up a round of golf, to burn up last night's rigatoni and clams.

We run to deny time's way with us and yet affirm our place in the great cycle of life. "In other words, we run," says a writer friend, "so we can escape the bear behind us."

The bear is all the predators that have made us both fearful and fleet; the bear is those aspects of our lives that drag us down and crush our skulls: all our physical decay, our weakening, our waning abilities, our dulling appetites,

1968: Nike, then called Blue Ribbon Sports, introduces Cortez running shoe for Mexico City games

1972: Bowerman pours polyurethane into a waffle iron for shoes used in Munich

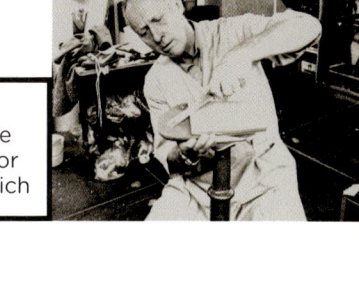

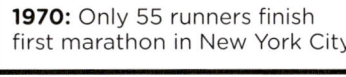

1970: Only 55 runners finish first marathon in New York City

1975: American running hero Steve Prefontaine, 24, killed in car accident, owning every national record from 2,000m to 10,000m and 2 miles to 6 miles

our growing depressions. We run to stay out in front of all that. Knowing this, we can sometimes even negotiate a truce and stop to share the blackberries on an August afternoon.

In every case, when we cross over from thought to action, when we're running out of fear or for joy-bam!-we are back on the savanna, all senses sharpened. A runner's high? No. A runner's jolt certainly, but the term suggests opiated dreaminess. It's really a runner's concentration, a runner putting aside the inconsequential.

We run to escape our mundane, appearances-driven waste of pure, timeless time. We run to be. We run to wildly flee from orthodoxy, expectation. We escape, as hunters do, to the things of the field, the woods, the pheasants exploding upward, scrawking like creaky gates.

At times we run to be absolutely alone, and yet are willing to be part of astounding masses, such as The Nike+ Human Race. This came as a shock to me. My first marathon, the 1963 Northwest AAU, had nine entrants. We imagined ourselves asocial eccentrics, so rare and lean and wacko that we epitomized the loneliness of the long distance runner. But in the 1970s, running boomed, and it seemed everybody found they could do a marathon

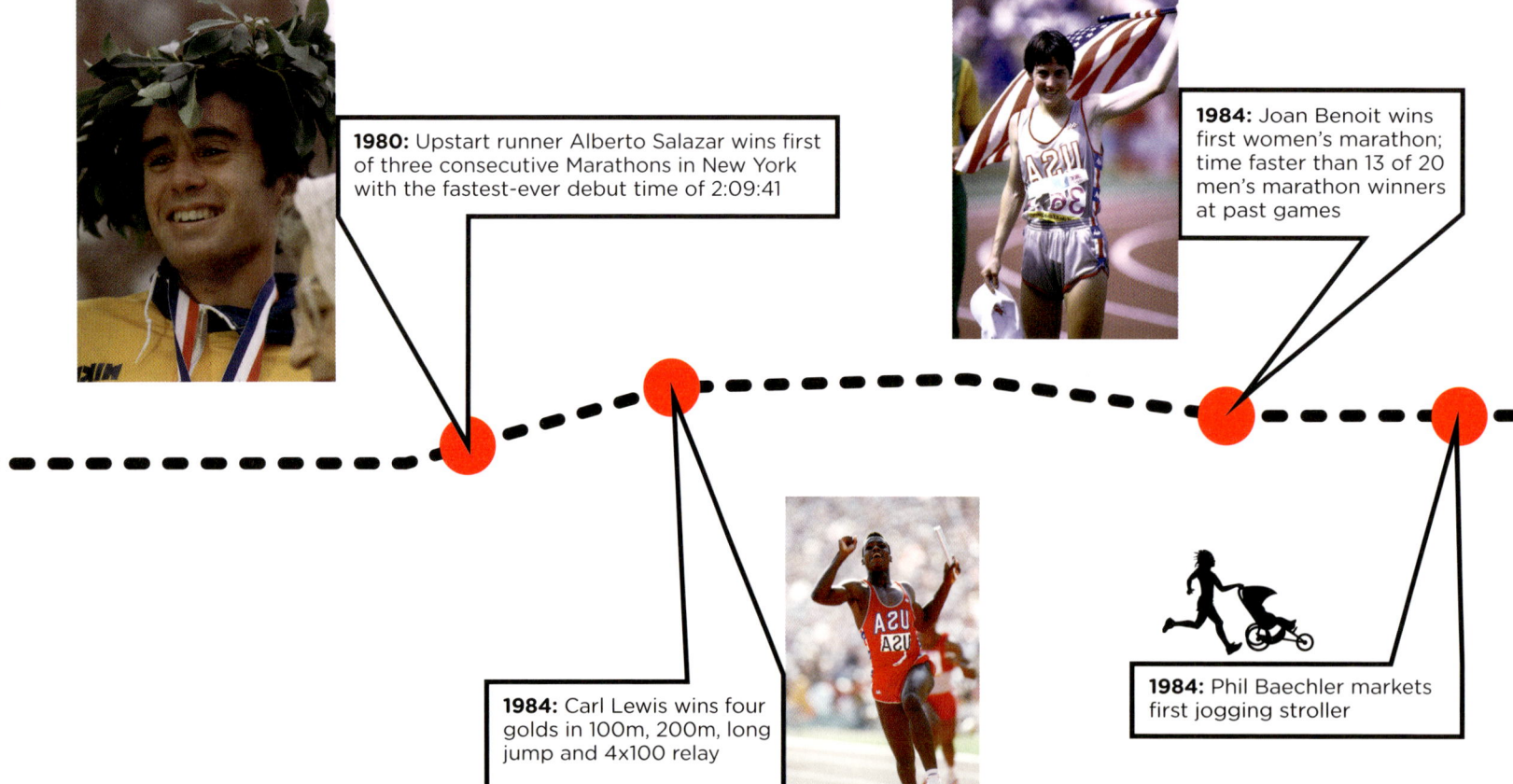

1980: Upstart runner Alberto Salazar wins first of three consecutive Marathons in New York with the fastest-ever debut time of 2:09:41

1984: Joan Benoit wins first women's marathon; time faster than 13 of 20 men's marathon winners at past games

1984: Carl Lewis wins four golds in 100m, 200m, long jump and 4x100 relay

1984: Phil Baechler markets first jogging stroller

if they paced themselves. Everybody found the hunter within. When the Honolulu Marathon got 97 percent of its 35,000 entrants to finish, no one was going to be lonely any more.

The reason for running that is most deeply lodged in history is to carry the word, the connecting word. Runner couriers made it possible for the federations of the early Greeks and Iroquois to function and thrive. Our most mythic racing distance is the 26 miles Pheidippides crossed to Athens after the battle of Marathon to tell his city they had defeated the invading Persians. "Rejoice!" he cried, before falling dead. "Rejoice, we conquer!"

We run, then, to obey Pheidippides and bear his message onward. We rejoice when athletes conquer themselves during supreme effort. We rejoice in knowing there is more honor in outrunning a man than killing him. We rejoice in having come so far from the savannah, and yet being always so near.

—Kenny Moore,
Champion Distance Runner

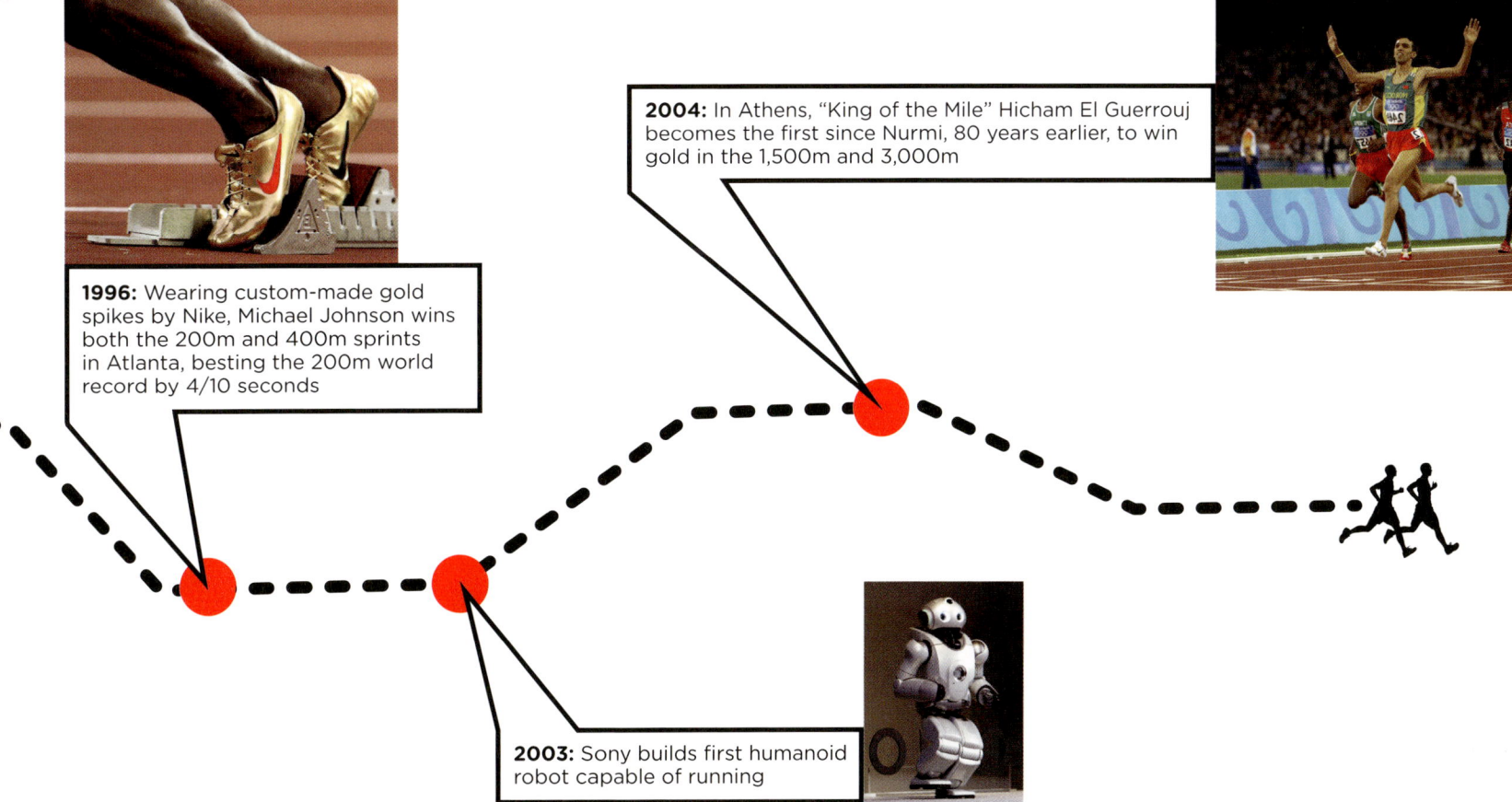

1996: Wearing custom-made gold spikes by Nike, Michael Johnson wins both the 200m and 400m sprints in Atlanta, besting the 200m world record by 4/10 seconds

2004: In Athens, "King of the Mile" Hicham El Guerrouj becomes the first since Nurmi, 80 years earlier, to win gold in the 1,500m and 3,000m

2003: Sony builds first humanoid robot capable of running

CITY COURSE MAPS

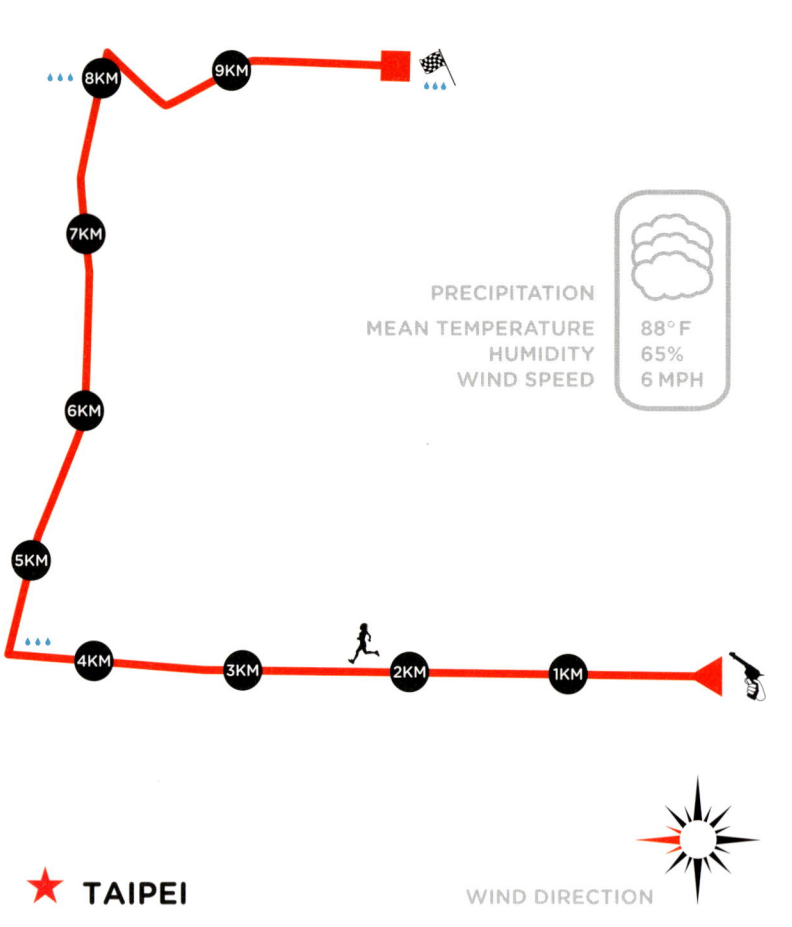

★ TAIPEI

PRECIPITATION
MEAN TEMPERATURE 88° F
HUMIDITY 65%
WIND SPEED 6 MPH

WIND DIRECTION

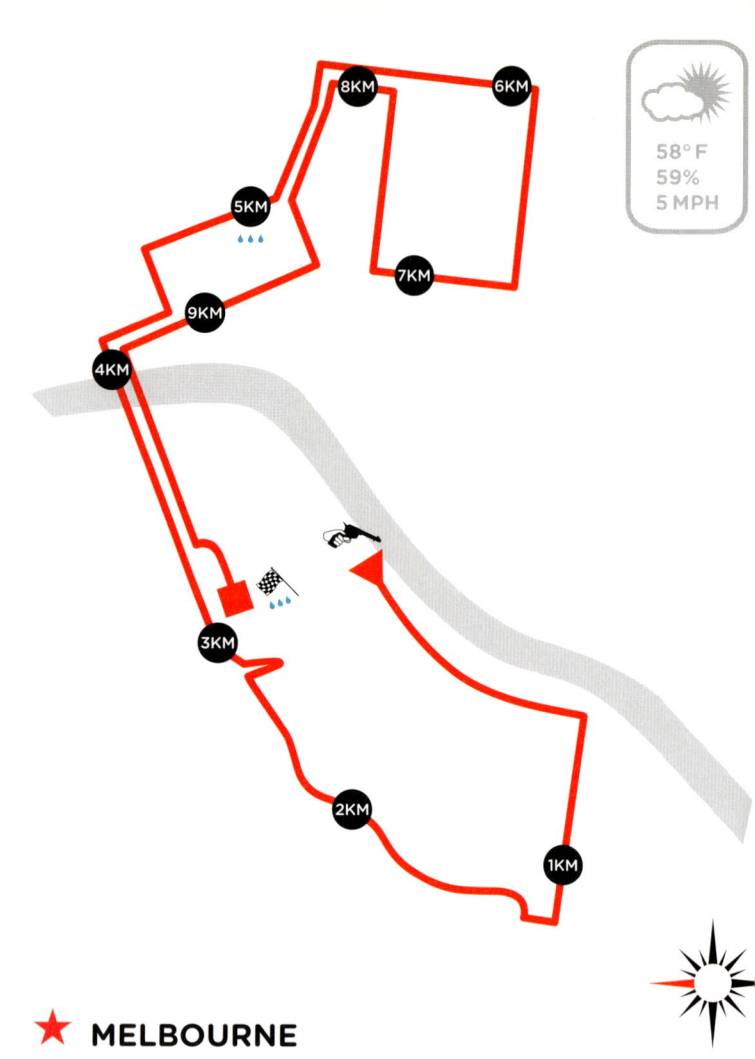

★ MELBOURNE

58° F
59%
5 MPH

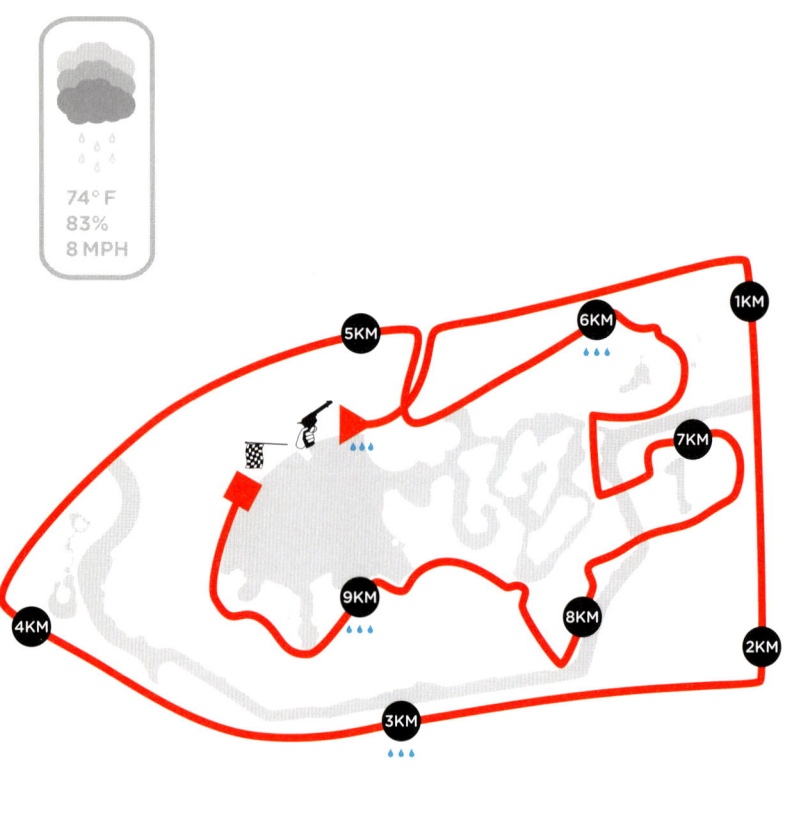

★ SHANGHAI

74° F
83%
8 MPH

★ MT. FUJI

71° F
87%
3 MPH

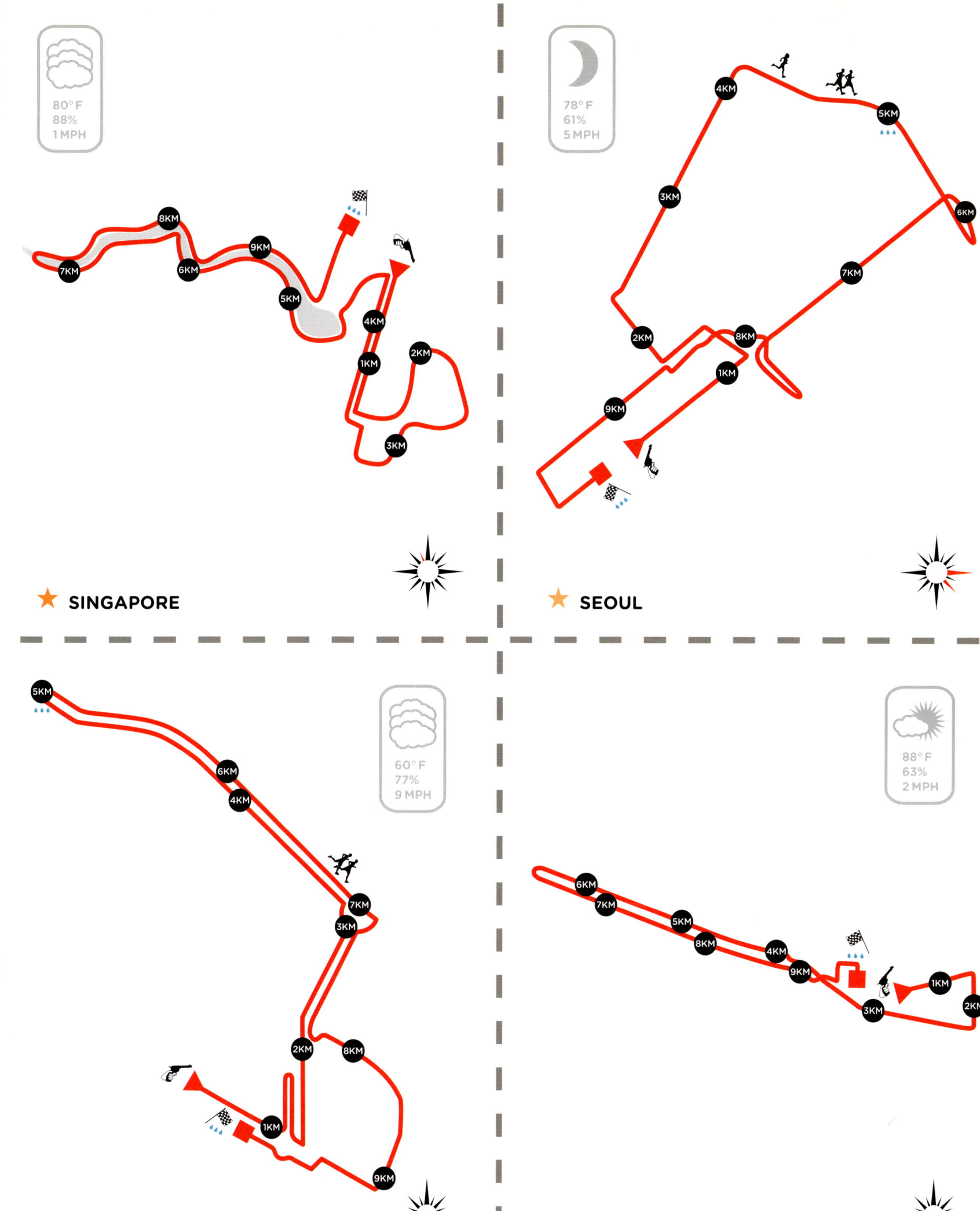

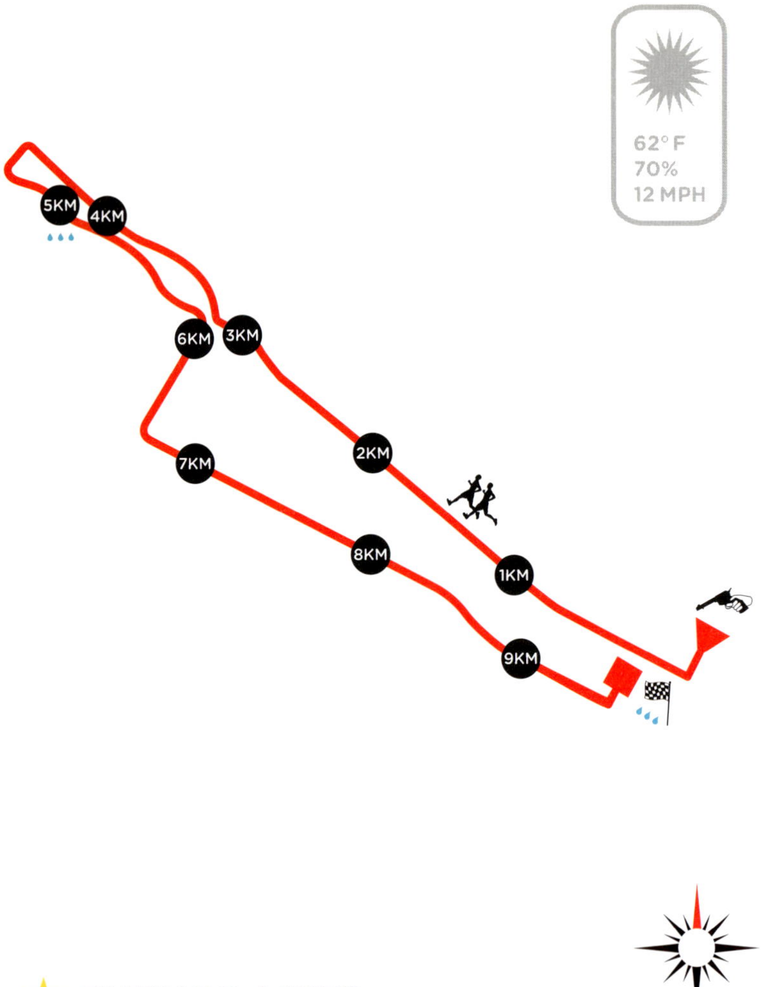

★ BUENOS AIRES

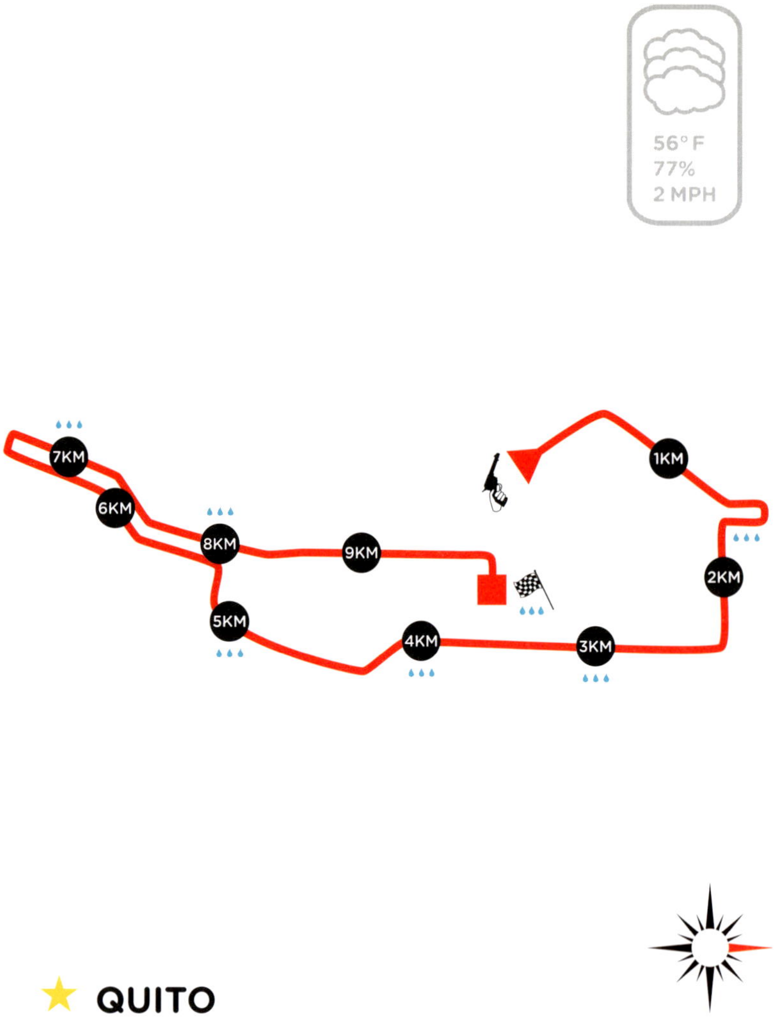

★ QUITO

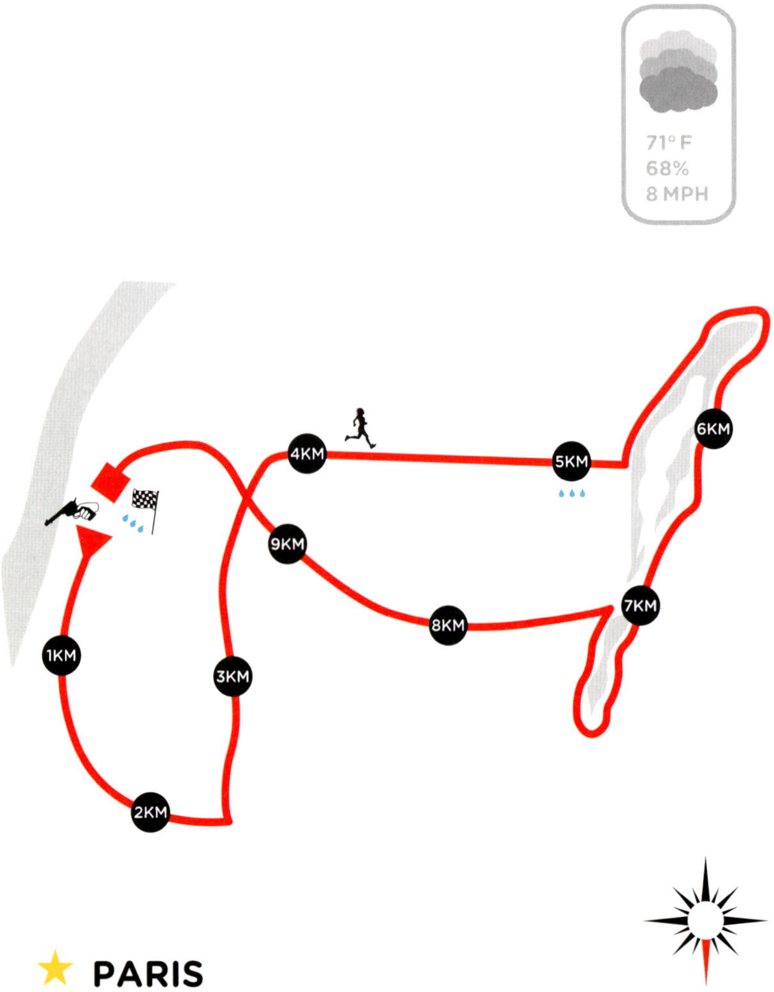

★ PARIS

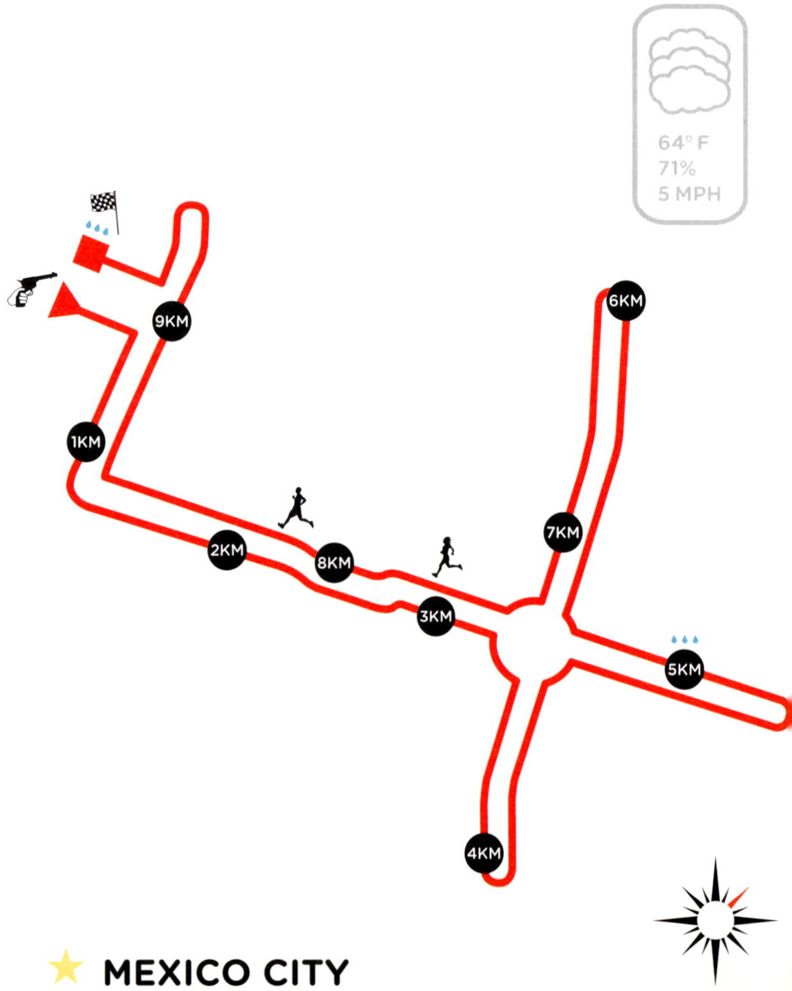

★ MEXICO CITY

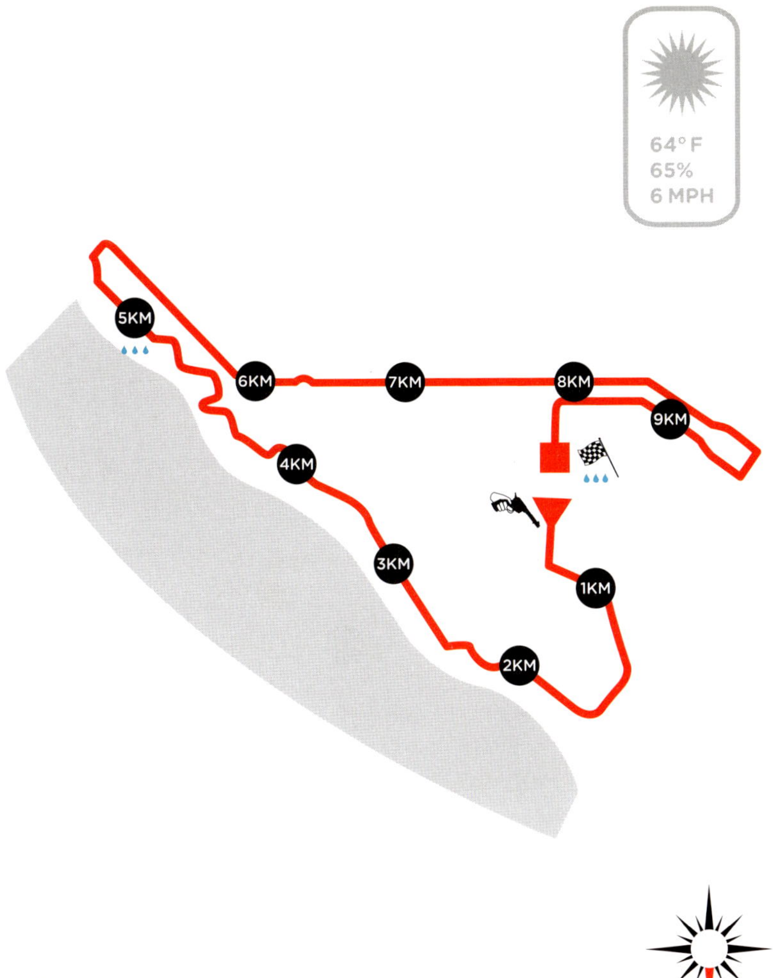

★ LIMA

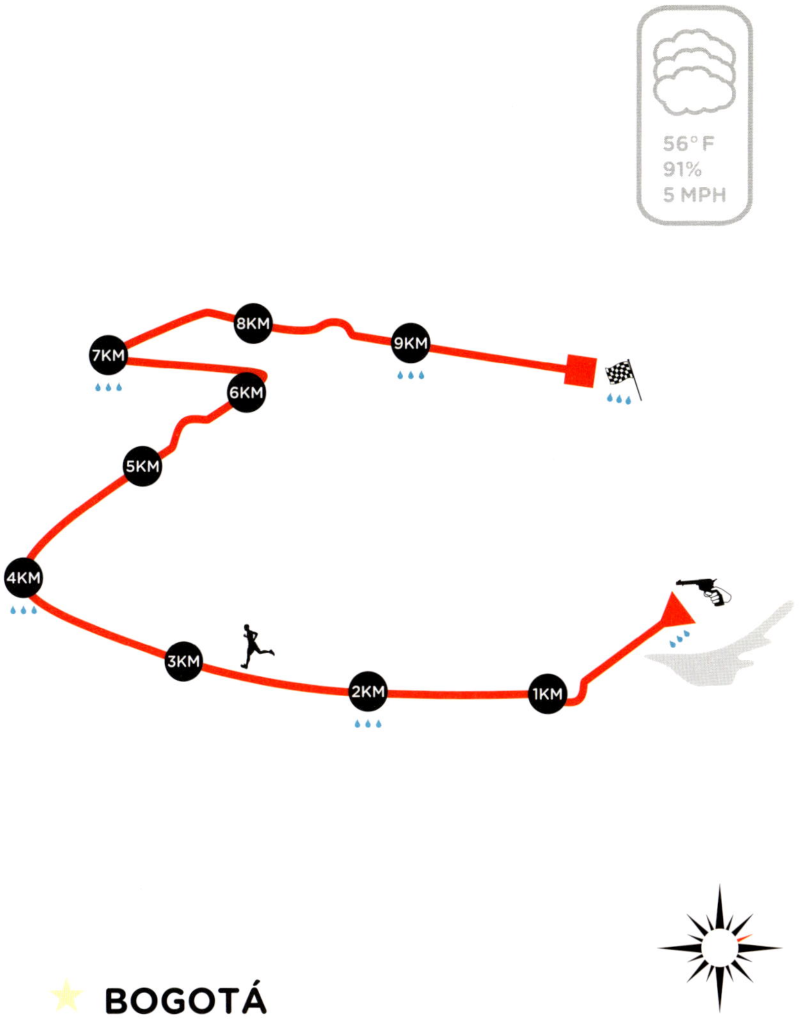

★ BOGOTÁ

★ WARSAW

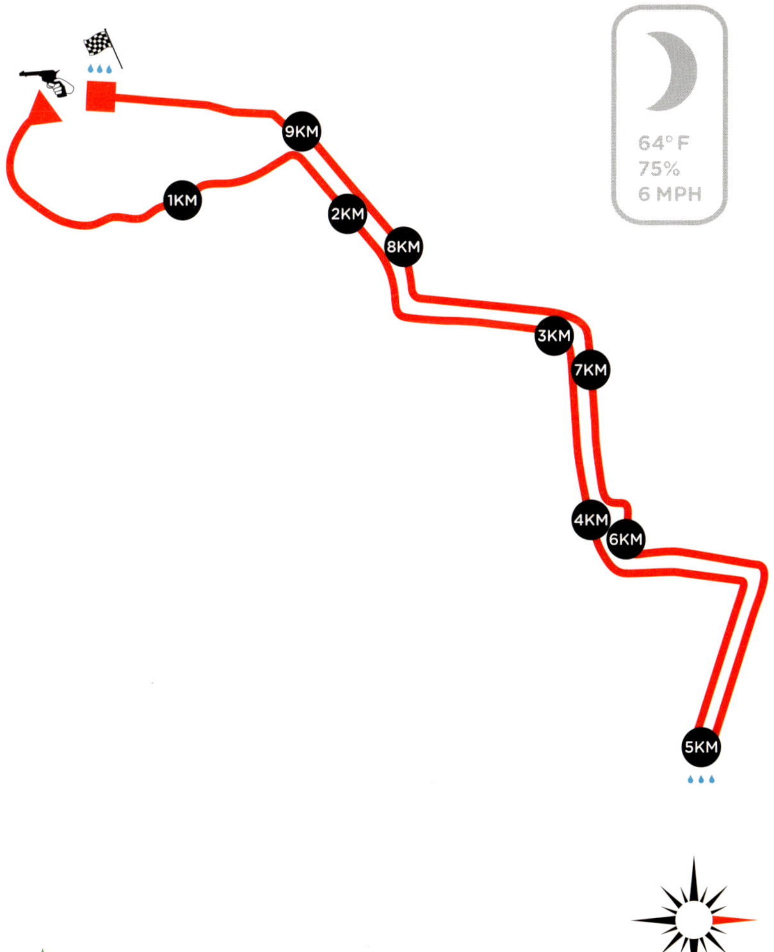

★ MUNICH

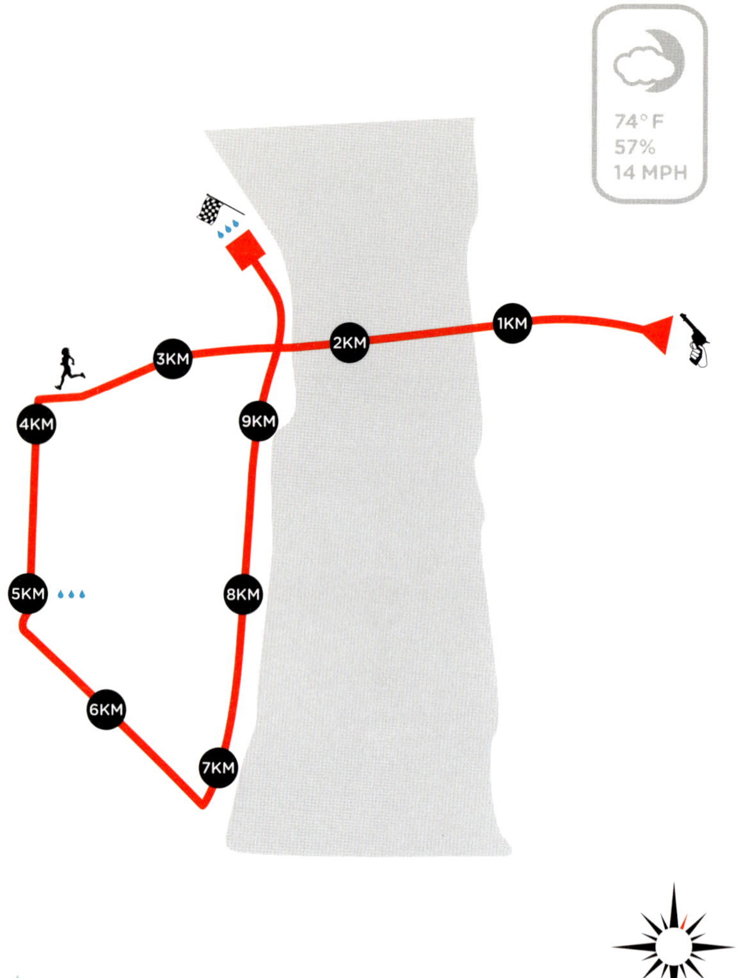

★ ISTANBUL

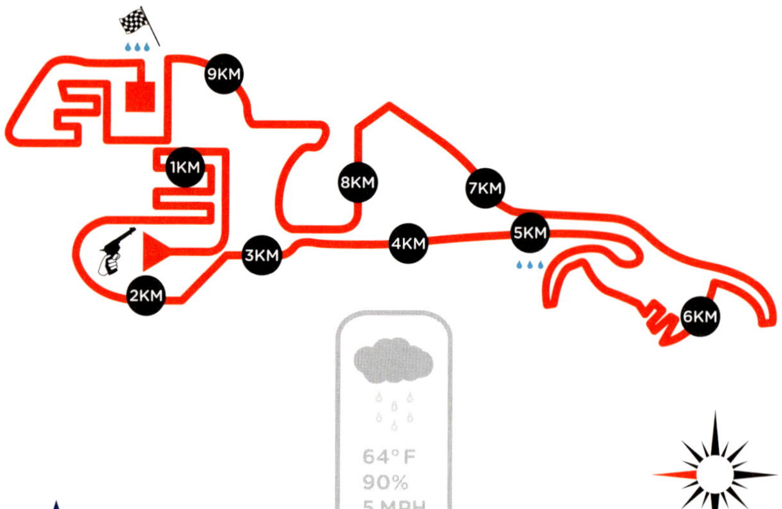

★ LONDON

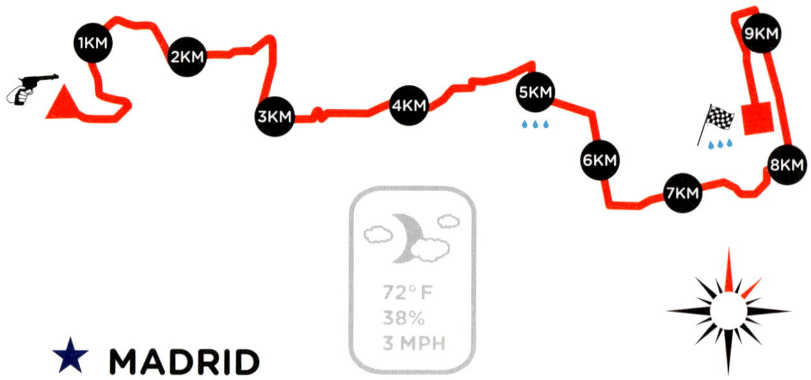

★ MADRID

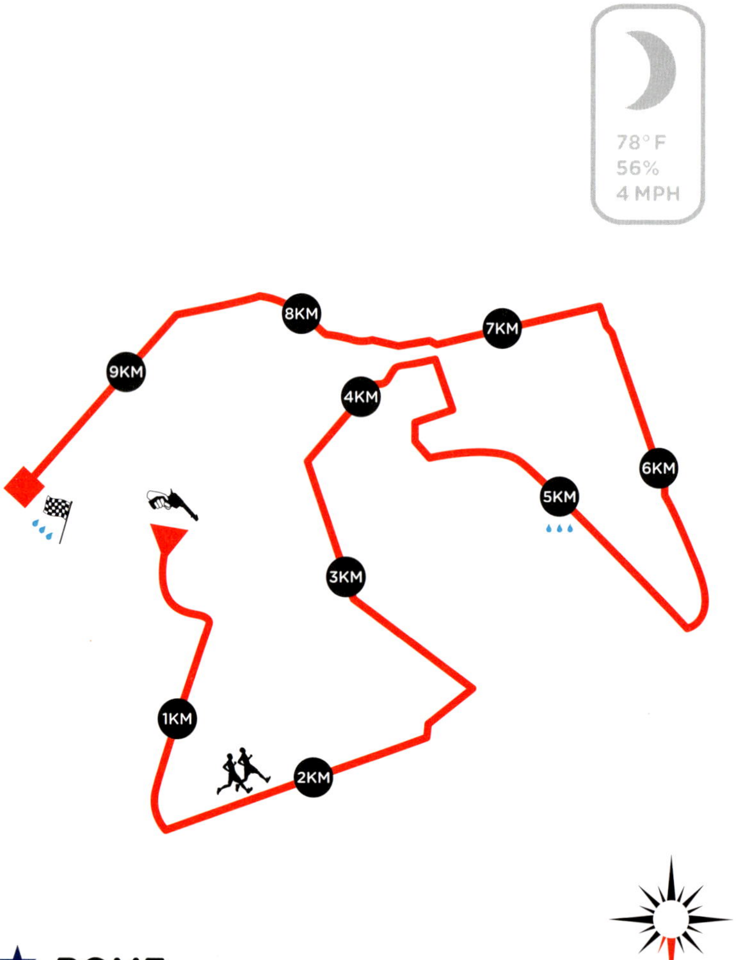

★ ROME

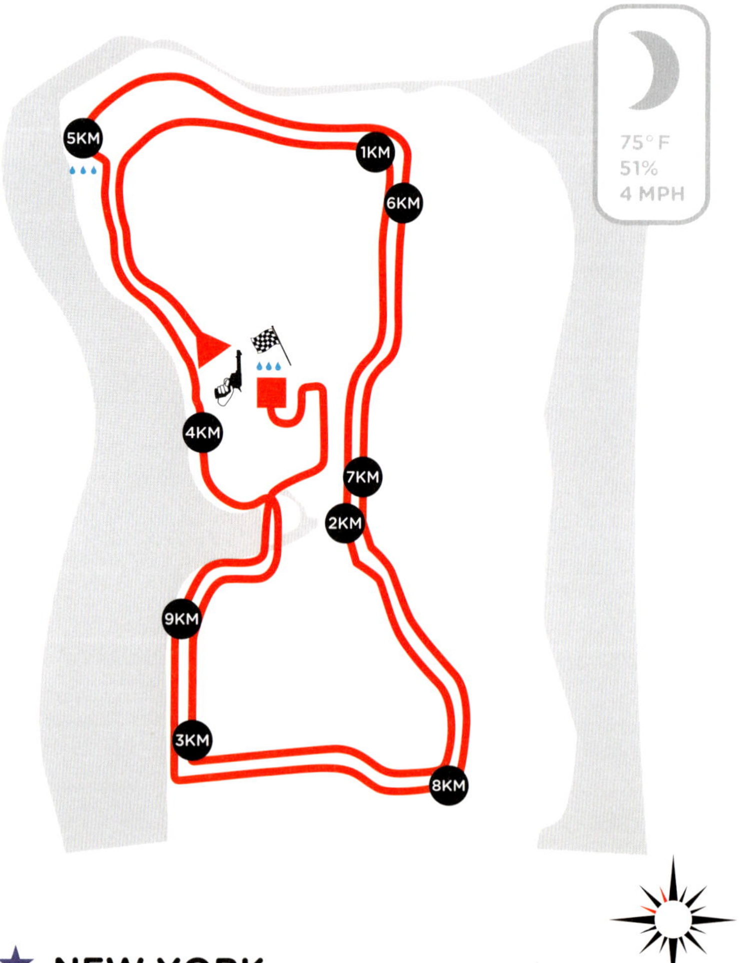

★ NEW YORK

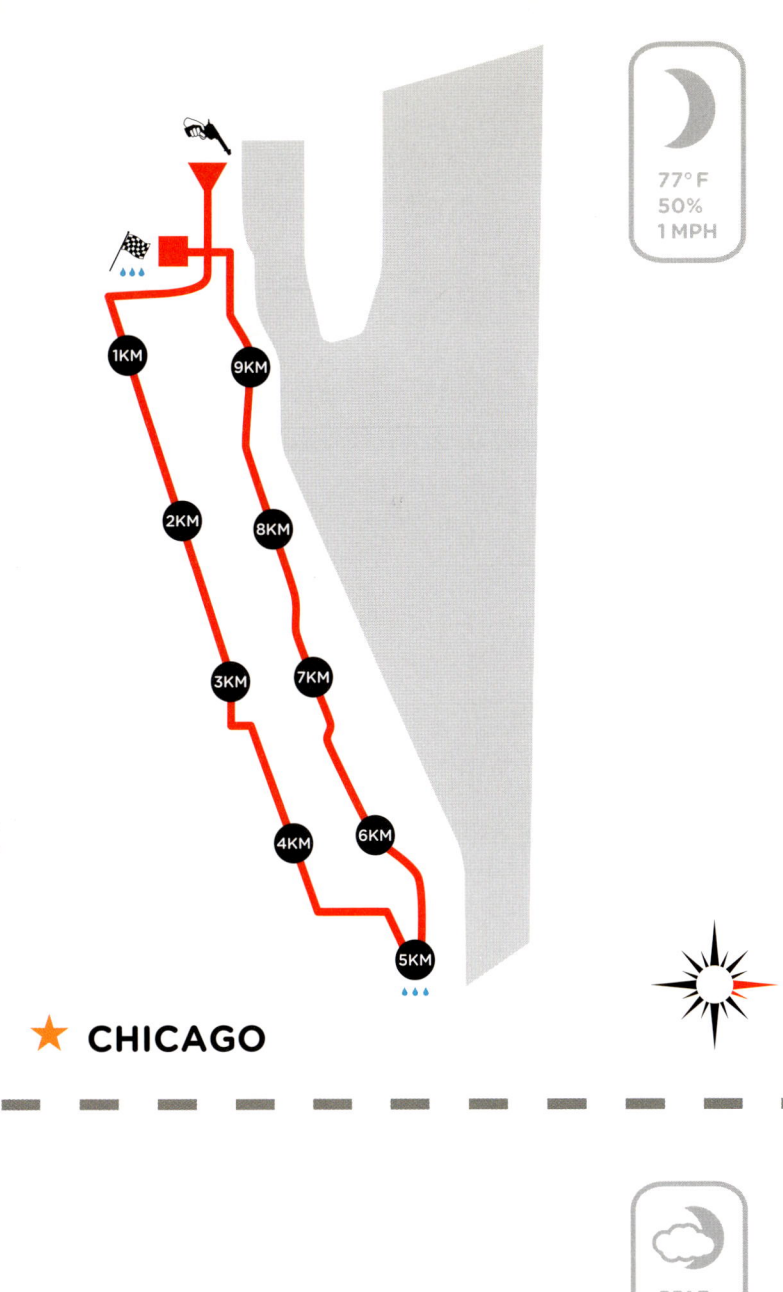
★ CHICAGO

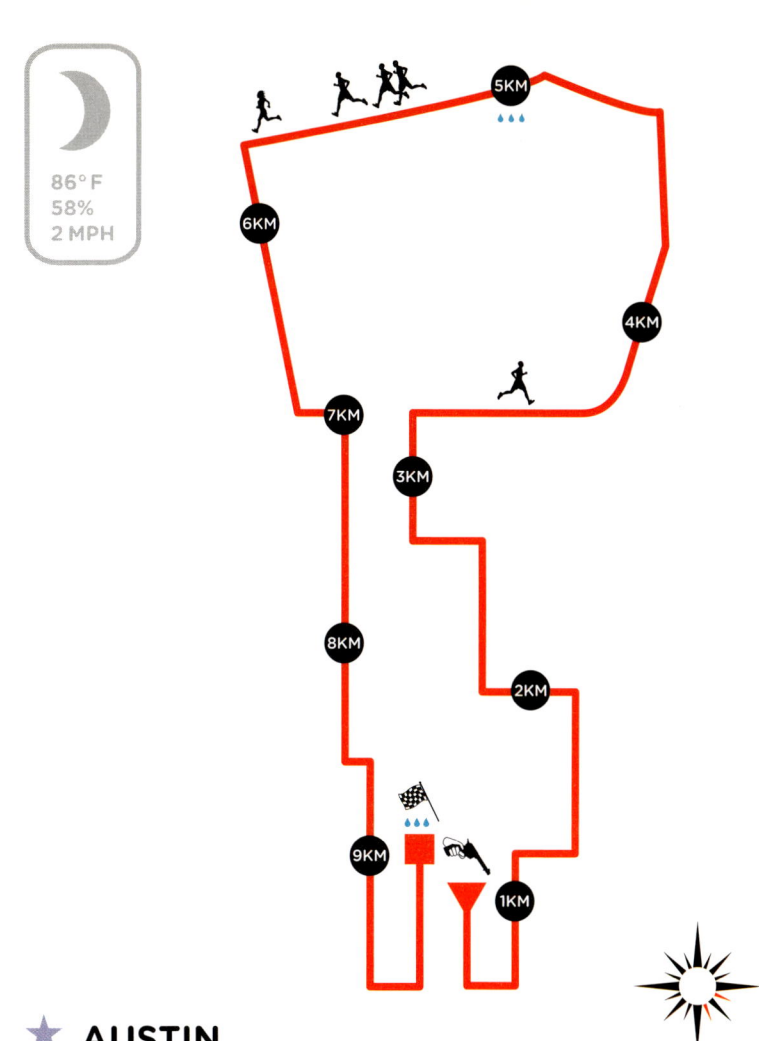
★ AUSTIN

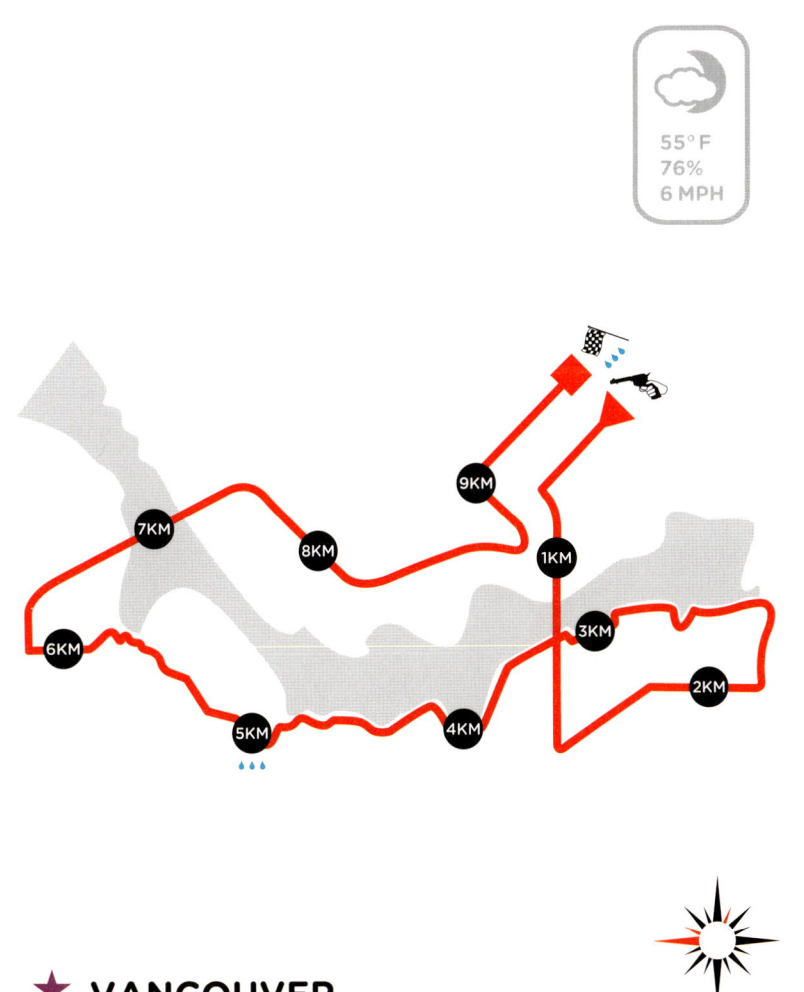
★ VANCOUVER

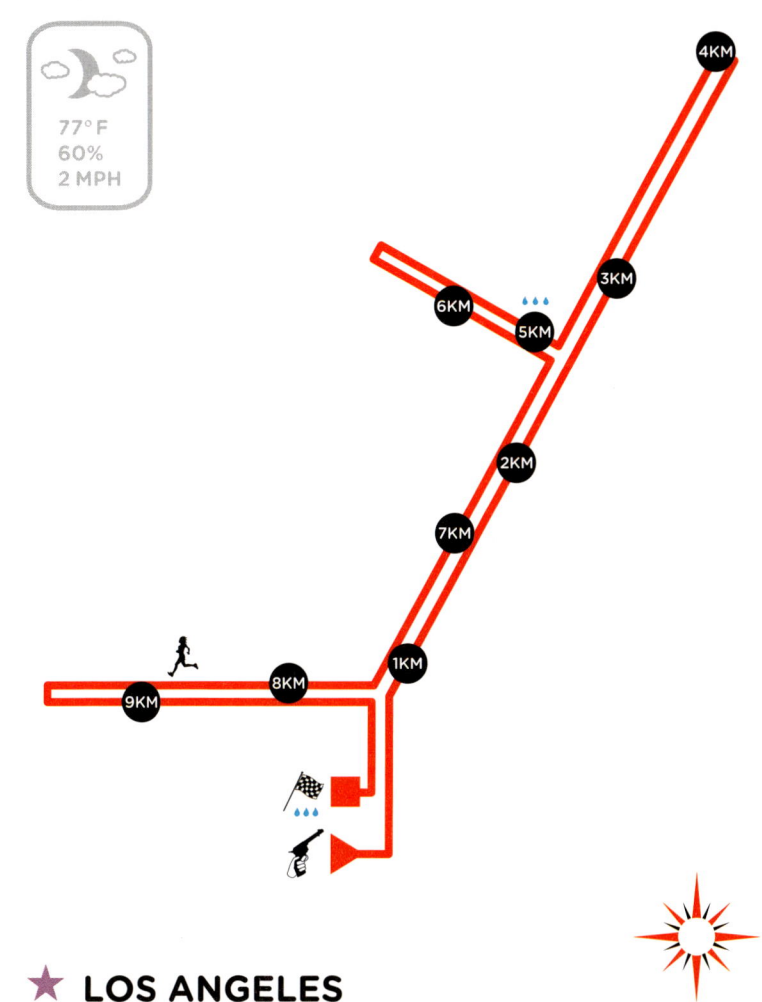
★ LOS ANGELES

ABOUT THE WRITERS

Alberto Salazar

Born in Havana, Cuba, Alberto Salazar was raised in Wayland, Massachusetts, and in 1976 moved to Eugene, Oregon, to attend the University of Oregon. While winning three straight New York Marathons from 1980 to 1982, he also broke the world record for the 5-mile distance and set new marathon marks in New York and Boston. Today he serves as a coach and mentor to many young up-and-coming athletes from around the world.

Don Kardong

Don Kardong's running career, which began in 1964 when he was a high school sophomore, included track and cross-country competition at Stanford University, and reached its apex at the marathon in Montreal, where he finished fourth. He has written extensively for *Running, Running Times, The Runner* and *Runner's World* magazines, and currently serves as Race Director of the Lilac Bloomsday Run in Spokane, Washington.

E. Casey Kittrell

E. Casey Kittrell is an editor at University of Texas Press in Austin. He runs about 20 miles a week.

Franz Lidz

Franz Lidz, a contributing editor at *Condé Nast Portfolio,* was a senior writer for *Sports Illustrated* for 27 years. He is the author of *Unstrung Heroes, Ghosty Men* and *Fairway To Hell.* He lives on a six-acre farm in Pennsylvania's Brandywine Valley with 25 chickens, 14 guinea fowl, two dogs, two cats and one wife.

Kenny Moore

Kenny Moore, a former world-class marathoner, is a longtime *Sports Illustrated* and *Runner's World* contributor. He is the biographer of Oregon track coach and Nike cofounder Bill Bowerman, and cowrote the films *Without Limits* and *Fire on the Track*, about Steve Prefontaine.

ABOUT THE CHARITIES

LIVESTRONG
LANCE ARMSTRONG FOUNDATION

Founded in 1997 by cancer survivor and champion cyclist Lance Armstrong, the Lance Armstrong Foundation (LAF) unites people to fight cancer. The LAF empowers cancer survivors to live life on their own terms and raises funds for the global fight against cancer. The LAF is committed to making cancer a global priority, raising cancer awareness and reducing the stigma associated with cancer. Unite and fight cancer at LIVE**STRONG**.org.

The **United Nations refugee agency** provides protection and assistance to the world's refugees. The agency began work in 1951 and since then has helped more than 50 million people successfully restart their lives, earning two Nobel Peace Prizes in the process—in 1954 and 1981. The **nine**million.org campaign was created in June 2006 to give more than nine million refugee children access to education, sport, and technology. The campaign highlights the potential of all refugee children and helps them to see beyond their current situation and envision a brighter future for themselves and their communities.

WWF is the world's largest conservation organization, working in 100 countries for nearly half a century. With the support of almost 5 million members worldwide, WWF is dedicated to delivering science-based solutions to preserve the diversity and abundance of life on Earth, stop the degradation of the environment and combat climate change. Visit www.wwf.org to learn more.

PHOTO CREDITS

front endpaper:	©Nike
back, front endpaper:	Laura Leon
p. 1:	©Nike
p. 2-3:	Janet Jarman/Getty Images
p. 6-7:	Karla Gachet/POLARIS
p. 8:	top, Quinn Rooney/Getty Images; bottom, Michael Grecco
p. 9:	top, Daniel Etter/Aurora; bottom, Quinn Rooney/Getty Images
p. 12-13:	Ana Nance/Redux
p. 16-17:	Nicolas Villaume/Aurora
p. 18:	Chicago, David Banks/SportPics; Istanbul, ©Nike; Buenos Aires, Nicolas Goldberg/POLARIS; London, Phil Cole/Getty Images; Mount Fuji, ©Nike; Melbourne, ©Nike
p. 19:	Rome, Stefano Dal Pozzolo/Contrasto/Redux; Madrid, ©Nike; Austin, Benjamin Sklar; Seoul, ©Nike; Paris, ©Presse Sports
p. 20:	Caracas, Gabriel Osorio/POLARIS; Vancouver, ©Nike; Shanghai, ©Nike; Munich, ©Nike; Warsaw, ©Nike; Mexico City, ©Nike
p. 21:	Lima, ©Nike; Taipai, ©Nike; Quito, ©Nike; São Paulo, Paulo Fridman; Bogotá, ©Nike; Singapore, ©Nike; Los Angeles, ©2008 adh photo; New York, Susan Goldman
p. 26:	top, Paulo Fridman; bottom, Stéphane Ruet/POLARIS
p. 27:	top, Nicolas Goldberg/POLARIS; bottom, Piotr Malecki/Getty Images
p. 34-35:	Matthew Mahon
p. 36:	Jesse Marlow/Oculi/Redux
p. 37:	Janet Jarman/Getty Images
p. 38-39:	Toru Yokota/onasia.com
p. 40:	clockwise from top: Stéphane Ruet/POLARIS; Andrew Lichtenstein/POLARIS
p. 41:	clockwise from top right: Gerhard Heidorn/Laif/Redux; Toru Yokota/onasia.com; Saverio Truglia
p. 42-43:	Thomas Michael Alleman
p. 44-45:	Kevin J Miyazaki/Redux
p. 46:	Seokyong Lee/POLARIS
p. 47:	www.kreutzphotography.com
p. 48-49:	Nicolas Villaume/Aurora
p. 50:	Kerem Uzel/NAR/Redux
p. 51:	Philip Gostelow/Aurora
p. 52-55:	Jeff Vinnick/POLARIS
p. 56-57:	Stuart Freedman/Aurora
p. 59:	Scott Dalton/POLARIS
p. 60-61:	Norman Ng/onasia.com
p. 62-63:	Robert Gallagher
p. 64-65:	Tommaso Bonaventura/Contrasto/Redux
p. 67:	Susana Raab/Aurora
p. 68-69:	Nicolas Villaume/Aurora
p. 70-71:	Ralph Talmont/Aurora
p. 72-73:	Ty Milford/Aurora
p. 74-75:	Marcos López/Aurora
p. 76-77:	Karla Gachet/POLARIS
p. 78-79:	Massimo Siragusa/Contrasto/Redux
p. 80:	Ana Nance/Redux
p. 81:	Nicolas Villaume/Aurora
p. 82-83:	Seokyong Lee/POLARIS
p. 85:	Craig Blankenhorn
p. 86:	Claudio Edinger
p. 87:	Christopher Morris/Redux
p. 88-89:	Narayan Mahon/POLARIS
p. 90-91:	Francesco Spotorno/Aurora
p. 93:	Jonathan Sprague/Redux
p. 98:	Narayan Mahon/POLARIS
p. 99:	©Nike
p. 100:	Kerem Uzel/NAR/Redux
p. 101:	Stéphane Ruet/POLARIS
p. 102-103:	Christopher Morris/Redux
p. 104-107:	Mark Peterson/Redux
p. 110-111:	Stéphane Ruet/POLARIS
p. 112-113:	Ivan Kashinsky/Aurora
p. 114-115:	Marcos López/Aurora
p. 116-117:	J Carrier
p. 118:	Philip Gostelow/Aurora
p. 119:	Benjamin Sklar
p. 120:	Francesco Spotorno/Aurora
p. 121:	Benjamin Sklar
p. 122-123:	PiChi Chuang
p. 124-125:	Paulo Fridman
p. 126-127:	Courtesy Tim Wiens; inset, Jeff Vinnick/POLARIS
p. 129:	Matt Eich/Aurora
p. 130:	Gabriel Osorio/POLARIS
p. 131:	Mark Asnin/Redux
p. 132-133:	Daniel Etter/Aurora
p. 134-135:	Susan Goldman
p. 136:	top, PiChi Chuang; bottom, David Butow/Redux
p. 137:	top, Samuel Aranda/POLARIS; bottom, Francesco Spotorno/Aurora
p. 138-139:	www.kreutzphotography.com

p. 140-141:	Nicolas Villaume/Aurora
p. 142-143:	Alain Buu/POLARIS
p. 145:	Candace Feit/POLARIS
p. 146-147:	Sandy Nicholson/Redux
p. 148-149:	Ralph Talmont/Aurora
p. 150:	Alexander von Spreti/Aurora
p. 151:	Daniel Etter/Aurora
p. 152:	Beth Rooney/Aurora
p. 153:	Adriana Zehbrauskas/POLARIS
p. 154:	clockwise from top: Will van Overbeek; PiChi Chuang; Phil Cole/Getty Images; Craig Blankenhorn; Eric Grigorian/POLARIS
p. 155:	clockwise from top right: Sharron Lovell/POLARIS; Eric Grigorian/POLARIS; Gabriel Osorio/POLARIS; Norman Ng/onasia.com; Alejandro Balaguer/Archivolatino/Redux
p. 156:	Seokyong Lee/POLARIS
p. 157:	Stephen Ferry/Redux
p. 158-159:	Andrew Lichtenstein/POLARIS
p. 160-163:	Tom Van Cakenberghe/onasia.com
p. 166-167:	Holly Reed
p. 168:	Francesco Spotorno/Aurora
p. 169:	Jesse Marlow/Oculi/Redux
p. 170-171:	PiChi Chuang
p. 173:	Rueven Kopitchinski/Getty Images
p. 174-175:	Gerhard Heidorn/Laif/Redux
p. 176-177:	Craig Blankenhorn
p. 178-179:	Stefano Dal Pozzolo/Contrasto/Redux
p. 180:	Adriana Zehbrauskas /POLARIS
p. 181:	Seokyong Lee/POLARIS
p. 182:	©George Butler/White Mtn Films
p. 183:	Susana Raab/Aurora
p. 184-185:	Nicolas Villaume/Aurora
p. 186-187:	Phil Cole/Getty Images
p. 188:	Sally Ryan/POLARIS
p. 189:	Christina Watts
p. 190-191:	Adriana Zehbrauskas/POLARIS
p. 192-193:	Jonathan Sprague/Redux
p. 195:	Robert Gallagher
p. 197:	Katja Heinemann/Aurora
p. 198-199:	clockwise from top: Marcos López/Aurora; Claudia Guadarrama/POLARIS; Stefano Dal Pozzolo/Contrasto/Redux; PiChi Chuang
p. 201:	Angela Smith/Redux
p. 203:	Benjamin Sklar
p. 205:	clockwise from top right: Benjamin Sklar; Brent Humphreys/Redux; Benjamin Sklar
p. 206:	Brent Humphreys/Redux
p. 207:	clockwise from top: Brent Humphreys/Redux; Brent Humphreys/Redux; Brent Humphreys/Redux; Benjamin Sklar
p. 208:	top, Christopher Morris/Redux; bottom, Alejandro Balaguer/Redux
p. 209:	top, Al Bello; bottom, Stéphane Ruet/POLARIS
p. 210-211:	Carlos Villallon/Redux
p. 218-219:	Alejandro Balaguer/Redux
p. 220:	top, Ivan Kashinsky/Aurora; bottom, Eric Grigorian/POLARIS
p. 221:	top, Quinn Rooney/Getty Images; bottom, Seokyong Lee/POLARIS
p. 222:	clockwise from top right: Ana Nance/Redux; Ana Nance/Redux; Saverio Truglia; Clay McLachlan/Aurora
p. 223:	clockwise from top right: Norman Ng/onasia.com; Piotr Malecki/Getty Images; Paulo Fridman; Massimo Siragusa/Contrasto/Redux; Jesse Marlow/Oculi/Redux; Ivan Kashinsky/Aurora; Angela Smith/Redux; ©Nike
p. 224-225:	Narayan Mahon/POLARIS
p. 226-227:	Kerem Uzel/NAR/Redux
p. 228-229:	Angela Smith/Redux
p. 230:	©2008 adh photo
p. 231:	clockwise from top right: ©2008 adh photo; Robson Muzel; ©2008 adh photo; ©2008 adh photo
p. 232:	Michael Grecco
p. 233:	clockwise from top right: Karla Gachet/POLARIS; Craig Blankenhorn; Karla Gachet/POLARIS; Samuel Aranda/POLARIS; Phil Cole/Getty Images
p. 234:	Adriana Zehbrauskas/POLARIS
p. 235:	Claudia Guadarrama/POLARIS
p. 236-237:	Quinn Rooney/Getty Images
p. 238:	Tay Kay Chin/POLARIS
p. 239:	top, Norman Ng/onasia.com; bottom, Tay Kay Chin/POLARIS
p. 240:	Getty Images
p. 241:	All Getty Images except top right; top right, courtesy Bayer
p. 242:	top left, Getty Images; top right, ©Nike
p. 243:	All Getty Images except top left; top left, ©Nike
p. 244-245:	Getty Images
front/back endpapers:	Piotr Malecki/Getty Images
	©Nike

THANKS TO THE FOLLOWING CONTRIBUTORS

Photographers:

Thomas Michael Alleman, Samuel Aranda, Mark Asnin, Alejandro Balaguer, David Banks, Al Bello, Craig Blankenhorn, Tommaso Bonaventura, George Butler, David Butow, Alain Buu, Tom van Cakenberghe, J Carrier, Tay Kay Chin, Woohae Cho, PiChi Chuang, Phil Cole, Stefano Dal Pozzolo, Scott Dalton, David Deal, Claudio Edinger, Matt Eich, Daniel Etter, Candace Feit, Stephen Ferry, Deliizia Flaccavento, Stuart Freedman, Paulo Fridman, Karla Gachet, Robert Gallagher, Nicolas Goldberg, Susan Goldman, Philip Gostelow, Michael Grecco, Eric Grigorian, Claudia Guadarrama, Gerhard Heidorn, Katja Heinemann, Brent Humphreys, Janet Jarman, Ivan Kashinsky, Reuven Kopitchinski, Ziv Koren, Christopher LaMarca, Seokyong Lee, Laura Leon, Andrew Lichtenstein, Marcos López, Sharron Lovell, Narayan Mahon, Matthew Mahon, Piotr Malecki, Jesse Marlow, Clay McLachlan, Ty Milford, Kevin J Miyazaki, Christopher Morris, Ana Nance, Norman Ng, Sandy Nicholson, Mads Nissen, Gabriel Osorio, Mark Peterson, Susana Raab, Holly Reed, Beth Rooney, Quinn Rooney, Stéphane Ruet, Sally Ryan, Ryu Seung-Il, Massimo Siragusa, Benjamin Sklar, Angela Smith, Francesco Spotorno, Jonathan Sprague, Chung Sung-Jun, Ralph Talmont, Saverio Truglia, Kerem Uzel, Will van Overbeek, Carlos Villallon, Nicolas Villaume, Jeff Vinnick, Alexander von Spreti, Christina Watts, CJ Sameer Wadhwa, Steve Chen, Toru Yokota, Adriana Zehbrauskas

Writers:

Lisa Abend, Tony Azios, Robert Baker, Catherine Davis, Lorenzo Duque, Mike Elkin, Farrell Evans, Mona Gable, Georgia Getz, Ioan Grillo, Suzy Hansen, Mei-Ling Hopgood, Jeffrey Iverson, Don Kardong, Helen Kay, Jasmina Keleman, Peter Kononczuk, Stephan Kuffner, Paul Ladewski, Andrew Lawrence, Rick Lipsey, Michael McKenzie, Amir Mizroch, Kristen Mueller, Miriam Murphy, Suzanne Nam, Amanda Pateman, María Pérez-Plá Leoz, Andrei Postelnicu, George Quaraishi, Nick Sheridan, Art Stricklin, Natalie Tso, Andrea Zarate

Thanks also to all of The Nike+ Human Race global and regional teams, Katya Able, Lori Baird, Jack Boyt, Adam Bright, Sari Cantrell, Jay Colton, Denise Courtney, Daniel Del Valle, Jennifer Erwitt, Frank DeRose, Mandi Eberle, Kent Gedman, Barbara Gogan, Mick Greenwood, Wyeth Hansen, Haley Hughes, Chuck Isaacs, Hjalti Karlsson, Kevin Kerr, Neal Klein, Chris LaBelle, Dot McMahon, Ally Merkley, Parisa Morid, Takashi Okamoto, Bob Roe, Holly Rothman, Kim Shannon, Rick Smolan, Lindsey Stanberry, Shoshana Thaler, Peter Truskier, Grady Turner, Topher White, Jan Wilker, Betty Wong and Megan Worman